ANTON CHEKHOV

The Seagull

translated from the Russian by
MICHAEL FRAYN

with commentary and notes by
NICK WORRALL

METHUEN DRAMA

Methuen Drama Student Edition

10 9 8 7 6 5 4 3 2

This edition first published in the United Kingdom in 2002
by Methuen Publishing Ltd

Methuen Drama
A & C Black Publishers Limited
38 Soho Square
London W1D 3HB

Reissued with a new cover design and additional material in 2006

This translation of *The Seagull* first published in 1986 by Methuen London Ltd
Copyright © 1986, 1991 by Michael Frayn. Original work entitled *Chaika*

Commentary and notes copyright © 2002, 2006 by Nick Worrall

The rights of the authors to be identified as the authors
of these works have been asserted by them in accordance with the
Copyright, Designs and Patents Act, 1988

A CIP catalogue record for this book is available from the British Library

ISBN 978 0 413 77100 1

Typeset by Deltatype Ltd, Birkenhead, Merseyside
Printed and bound in Great Britain by Cox & Wyman Ltd, Reading, Berkshire

Caution
All rights whatsoever in this translation are strictly reserved,
and application for performance, etc., by professional or amateur companies
should be made to: the Peters Fraser & Dunlop Group Ltd, Drury House,
34–43 Russell Street, London W2B 5HA. No performance
may be given unless a licence has been obtained.

This book is sold subject to the condition that it shall not,
by way of trade or otherwise, be lent, resold, hired out,
or otherwise circulated in any form of binding or cover
other than that in which it is published and without a
similar condition, including this condition, being
imposed on the subsequent purchaser.

Contents

Anton Chekhov: 1860–1904   v

Plot   xi

Commentary   xx
  The Seagull in context   xx
  The seagull and the enchanted lake   xxv
  The play-within-the-play   xxviii
  Time and memory; youth and age; sleep and dream   xxxiii
  Art and life; love and destruction   xxxvi
  Comedy or tragedy?   xxxix
  Problems of translation   xli
  Critical perspectives   xlvi
  The Seagull in production   liv

Further Reading   lxxvii

Translator's Introduction   lxxix

A Note on the Translation   xciii

Pronunciation of the Names   xcvii

THE SEAGULL   1

Notes   68

Questions for Further Study   91

Anton Chekhov: 1860–1904

1860 Born, the grandson of a serf and third son of the merchant grocer Pavel Yegorovich Chekhov and his wife Yevgeniya Yakovlevna Morozova, in Taganrog, a small southern port on the Sea of Azov, where he spends his first nineteen years.

1868 Enters the local *gimnaziya* or high school, where he acquires a reputation as a practical joker and is known as 'bomb-head' because of the over-developed size of his cranium.

1876 His father, bankrupt, flees from Taganrog concealed beneath a mat at the bottom of a cart. The family follow him to Moscow, leaving Chekhov behind to complete his schooling. Chekhov writes a short (2–3 pages) 'absurd' play, called *A Forced Declaration or The Sudden Death of a Horse, or The Magnanimity of the Russian People*.

1878 He writes a full-length play, and a vaudeville, *Why the Hen Clucks*, both now lost. The play, *Bezotsovshchina* (Fatherless/Without Patrimony) may be the one which later resurfaced, and is generally known as *Platonov*.

1879 Having completed his education, Chekhov moves to Moscow to join his family, now impoverished and living in a red-light district. He enters the medical faculty of Moscow University where he studies for the next five years.

1880 Begins contributing humorous stories to minor magazines under the pen-name, Antosha Chekhonte. His first short stories are published in the tenth issue of the magazine *Strekoza* (The Dragonfly).

1880 Chekhov writes for Moscow and St Petersburg comic
–87 magazines under various pseudonyms, 'A Doctor without Patients', 'A Man without a Spleen', 'My Brother's Brother', and others.

1881 He offers a full-length play to the Moscow Maly Theatre which is rejected. Presumed lost, a play is discovered in 1920, without a title, but containing plot elements which resemble those of the rejected work. It is most usually known as *Platonov*, after the play's central character. Because of its inordinate length, the play is usually acted in adapted or abbreviated versions – the most famous being Michael Frayn's *Wild Honey* (1984).

1884 Chekhov qualifies as a doctor and begins practising in the Moscow regions of Zvenigorod and Voskresensk – the start of a sporadic second career which, over the years, brings him much hard work and little income. Describing the relationship between his work as a doctor and that as a writer, he compares them to those between a man and his wife and a man and his mistress, respectively. His first collection of stories, *Fairy Tales of Melpomene*, is published, as is a three-page 'terrible-awful-disgraceful desperate t-r-r-rragedy', *Dishonourable Tragedians and Leprous Dramatists*. A 'dramatic study in one act', *On The High Road*, is rejected by the censor as 'a gloomy and sordid play'. He begins to show first signs of the tubercular condition which was to end his life twenty years later.

1885 Makes his first trip to St Petersburg where he meets and befriends Alexey Suvorin, millionaire proprietor of the newspaper *Novoye vremya* (The New Time), a man of reactionary views who has a concession on all the railway bookstalls in Russia.

1886 Begins writing for *Novoye vremya*. His second collection of short stories, *Motley Tales*, is published. He also writes two short one-acters – *Swan Song* and *On the Harmfulness of Tobacco*.

1887 First production of a full-length play, *Ivanov*, given on 19 November at the Korsh Theatre in Moscow. Despite only four rehearsals 'the play had a substantial success' with curtain calls after each act including one, following Act Two, for the author himself. The production was also hissed. According to Chekhov, the second performance '. . . didn't go badly . . . Again there were curtain calls after Act Three (twice) and after Act Four, but no hisses this time' (Letters to his brother, Alexander, dated 20 and 24 November 1887).

1888 Writes a long short story, 'The Steppe', which appears in one of the prestigious 'thick journals' *Russkaya mysl'* (Russian Thought) and which marks a change in Chekhov's attitude to his fiction writing, thanks largely to an appreciative letter from the literary critic, D. V. Grigorovich. Henceforth, Chekhov will write fewer stories and, generally, longer and more substantial ones. This year also sees the appearance of his best-known and most performed one-act 'jokes' – *The Bear* and *The Proposal*. At the première of the first, a samovar bursts on stage and scalds one of the actors. The Russian Academy awards Chekhov the Pushkin prize for a book of short stories, *In the Twilight*.

1889 Chekhov's full-length play, *The Wood Demon*, strongly influenced by Tolstoyan ideas, opens at the Abramova Theatre in Moscow but closes after only three performances. It will later reappear, in revised form, as *Uncle Vanya*. He writes two more short plays, *A Tragedian in Spite of Himself* and the more extended *The Wedding*.

1890 Sets out on a journey in unsprung carts over unsurfaced roads, as well as by train and steamer, to the convict settlement on the island of Sakhalin off Russia's eastern seaboard. The journey takes from 21 April to 11 July. Once there, Chekhov conducts a census of some 10,000 convicts, averaging 160 interviews a day as part of a three-month medical/statistical survey which includes the examination of living conditions among convicts and exiles, looking at school and library provision, etc. He also makes travel notes which are written up as nine articles for *Novoye vremya* and which become the basis of the documentary work, *The Island of Sakhalin*, published in 1895. He leaves Siberia on 13 October and returns by sea via Hong Kong (where he admires British colonial rule) and Ceylon (where he admires the beauty of the women), arriving in Odessa via the recently opened Suez Canal on 1 December.

1891 His one-act play *The Anniversary* staged. Makes his first trip to Western Europe in the company of Suvorin.

1892 He purchases an estate near Moscow, Melikhovo (now a Chekhov museum, as is his residence-cum-surgery in Moscow), where he and the remainder of his family move. During the course of this and the following year, Chekhov immerses himself in the struggle against the effects on the local population of famine and cholera. He also helps to build schools, plants fruit trees, cultivates fir, pine, larch and oak, grows flowers, stocks fishponds, and runs the estate as a self-supporting commune growing its own cereal and vegetables. His medical 'diocese' covers 26 villages. One of his best-known short stories, 'Ward 6', is published in November.

1894 His health worsens but, despite this, he travels to Europe again in the company of Suvorin.

1895 Chekhov's fame as a writer spreads. He meets Tolstoy for the first time.

1896 Sponsors the construction of a primary school in nearby Talezh. *The Seagull* is premièred unsuccessfully at the Alexandrinsky Theatre, St Petersburg. Chekhov vows never to write another play.

1897 Sponsors construction of a primary school in the neighbouring village of Novosyolki. Suffers a violent lung haemorrhage while dining with Suvorin and is diagnosed as suffering from tuberculosis. He is also plagued by piles, gastritis, migraine, dizzy spells, and palpitations of the heart (not unlike the comic protagonist, Lomov, in his one-act 'joke' *The Proposal*). A collection of his plays is published which includes *Uncle Vanya*.

1897 Wintering in Nice for his health, he becomes interested in
–98 the Dreyfus case and takes Zola's side in defence of the French officer. Relations cool with the rather anti-semitic Suvorin.

1898 Has a villa built in Yalta on the Black Sea (now a Chekhov museum) where weather conditions are better suited for his illness. Following the opening of the Moscow Art Theatre in October 1898, *The Seagull* is given its second, successful, première in December, produced by Stanislavsky and Nemirovich-Danchenko and with Olga Knipper as Arkadina and Stanislavsky as Trigorin.

1899 Sells Melikhovo and moves permanently to Yalta. Also sells the copyright on all his works, past, present and future, to the St Petersburg publisher, A. F. Marks, for 75,000 roubles. *Uncle Vanya* staged with tremendous success by the Moscow Art Theatre on 26 October, with Knipper as Yelena and Stanislavsky as Astrov. Chekhov begins corresponding with Knipper, whom he had admired at a rehearsal of *Tsar Fedor* in 1898 and whom he is to marry in 1901. One of his best-known short stories, 'Lady with Lapdog', is published. Having corresponded with Gorky, Chekhov meets him for the first time and is instrumental in getting the Art Theatre to perform Gorky's plays *The Merchant Class* and *The Lower Depths*.

1899–1902 Edits and publishes his *Complete Works* in eleven volumes.

1900 Elected to honorary membership of the Academy of Sciences. Works on *Three Sisters* with members of the Moscow Art Theatre in mind. Winters in Nice.

1901 *Three Sisters* premièred at the Art Theatre on 31 January with Knipper as Masha and Stanislavsky as Vershinin. A qualified success. On 25 May he marries Knipper and honeymoons in south-east Russia. Meetings with Leo Tolstoy, Maxim Gorky, Ivan Bunin and Alexander Kuprin.

1902 Resigns from the Academy of Sciences in protest at Gorky's expulsion from that institution for his radical beliefs.

1903 Second edition of his *Complete Works* published. Despite worsening health, he works on his final play, *The Cherry Orchard*, again with specific Moscow Art Theatre actors in mind.

1904 Première of *The Cherry Orchard* on 17 January. Chekhov is taken seriously ill in the spring. He and Knipper leave for the health resort of Badenweiler in the Black Forest area of Germany, where he dies on 2 July. His last words

are a request for champagne. His body is brought by rail
to Moscow in a waggon for frozen goods marked
'Oysters' and, on 9 July is interred in the cemetery of the
Novodevichy Monastery, where many of Russia's great
writers lie.

Plot

The action unfolds on the estate owned by Peter (Piotr) Sorin, a retired senior law-court official and brother to a wealthy egotistical actress, whose stage name is Arkadina, and who has an established reputation in the Russian provincial theatre, as well as a reputation for financial meanness where her relatives and employees are concerned. Other residents of the estate include her son, Konstantin, who has ambitions to become an avant-garde writer and who shows signs of a mother fixation. He also suffers from feelings of social inferiority stemming from his official status as son of 'a Kiev shopkeeper' – the occupation of his father who was also a well-known provincial actor. What has become of the father is unclear but, to his son's bitter chagrin, the mother has taken up with a 'famous' writer of realistic fiction, Boris Trigorin, whom she has brought for the summer to the Sorin estate, which is managed by Shamrayev, a rather cantankerous individual with a taste for opera and the theatre. A regular visitor to the estate over many years is the urbane and charming Dr Dorn, who is loved by Shamrayev's wife Polina, and who acts as a kind of protective father-figure to the group – ministering to the sick and nerve-worn, comforting the lovesick and lovelorn. Completing the group are a local school teacher, Medvedenko, a rather pedantic individual who is in love with Masha, the daughter of Shamrayev and Polina. Medvedenko's love for Masha is unrequited, as she is in love with Konstantin who, in his turn, is in love with Nina, the daughter of a wealthy landowner who lives on an adjoining estate on the other side of a lake which separates the two properties. Nina's life is dominated by her father (whom we never see) who, following the death of her mother has married again, and we learn that Nina lives unhappily with him and her stepmother, describing her life as a form of incarceration with brief periods of liberty. It is during one of these brief moments that she escapes to appear in a play which Konstantin has written. The work is a 'symbolist' drama about the World Soul, in which Nina is to play the only role in a performance staged on a roughly-constructed platform stage built out-of-doors and situated so that, when the curtain is raised, the audience will be able to see the real lake as a backdrop, lit by the rising moon. The poor reception of his play, combined with the failure of his relationship with Nina, leads to Konstantin's first attempt to kill himself (between Acts Two and Three). During Act Three, Nina compounds his distress by conceiving an infatuation for Trigorin, which also disturbs Konstantin's mother and leads to the departure from the estate of Arkadina and Trigorin, immediately followed by that of Nina, who agrees to meet Trigorin in Moscow. Act Four takes place two years later and recounts what has happened to Nina and Trigorin in the interim, including their brief affair, a child which died in infancy, Nina's abandonment by Trigorin and his reconciliation with Arkadina. Meanwhile Konstantin has developed a reputation as a writer and Sorin has grown increasingly enfeebled. During the act, all the protagonists are reunited on the estate, including Nina, who has returned to the area in search of her past. A final scene between Nina and Konstantin concludes with her departure for work in a provincial theatre and Konstantin's second, successful, attempt on his own life.

Act One
The play opens in a section of the park on Sorin's estate where Yakov, an estate servant, and his fellow workers are putting the finishing touches to an improvised stage and their hammering and coughing is in counterpoint to the opening conversation between Masha and Medvedenko about death, art, money and time, whilst Masha's habitual snuff-taking introduces one of several 'leitmotifs'[1] in the play. They are joined by a nervous Konstantin and his uncle, Sorin, the former

---

[1] *leitmotif*: a term which is derived from the music dramas of Richard Wagner but which can be used to describe any (non-musical) theme associated with a particular person, situation or sentiment and which recurs in recognisable variations throughout a dramatic work.

obsessed with punctuality, tidiness, himself, his mother, and
Nina; the latter preoccupied with country life (decidedly inferior
to town life), sleep, and howling dogs. Konstantin offers
conflicting views of his mother as jealous, mean and
superstitious whilst also capable of being a ministering angel.
He also conveys his views of dominant trends in the theatre of
the day, as well as his sense of a need for 'new forms'. Nina
arrives on horseback against a blood-red sunset having secured
half an hour's liberty and identifies herself, for the first time,
with a seagull and the lake: 'But it's the lake that draws me
here, like a seagull . . .' (p.7). It also becomes apparent that she
doesn't think much of Konstantin's play, which is timed for
moonrise at 8.30, and which according to Nina has no 'living
characters' or love interest in it (p.8). The audience arrives for
the start of the play and the talk is of health, age, theatre,
idealism and love. Dorn sings to himself some lines from the
first of a number of songs with which he punctuates the play's
action, whilst Arkadina and Konstantin exchange 'significant'
quotations from *Hamlet*, one of many intertextual references to
both this and other works. Konstantin's play begins with Nina,
dressed in a white garment, sitting on a rock in a 'void' and
describing what life will be like in 200,000 years' time. All
human and animal life will be extinct, yet the struggle between
Spirit and Matter will continue. The World Soul represents the
unity of consciousness and instinct in a world where matter is
in eternal flux and only spirit is constant. Ahead is the struggle
with the Devil – the Father of Eternal Matter – until the
triumph of Spirit heralds an age of harmony and the reign of
the Universal Will. These elevated abstractions are
accompanied, at a crucial point, by very crude stage effects
supplied by the estate workers which prompt derisory
comments from Arkadina, born of incomprehension,
insensitivity, possible jealousy, even a sense of threat, but also a
perception of the comic disunity between poetic aspiration and
practical realisation. Konstantin, in filial fury, brings the
performance to a premature close and storms off, seemingly
oblivious to any responses other than his mother's to both the
play and his display of childish petulance. Arkadina, in
typically egotistical fashion, interprets the play as an attack on

herself, whilst everyone else appears to have forgotten all about
Nina, who eventually emerges from behind the curtain and is
presented to the 'great writer', Trigorin. She is overawed and
hurries away to reach home by her appointed hour. Everyone
else exits, leaving Dorn to muse on certain positive qualities
which he feels the play possessed and to give the disconsolate
Konstantin some useful advice about needing a 'definite goal'
(p.18), which the latter is in no mood to receive. Impatiently,
Konstantin goes off in search of Nina, leaving Dorn in the
company of Masha, who confesses her love for Konstantin.
Dorn blames the 'spells woven by this lake' (p.19) and tenderly
states his powerlessness to help her in her tearful distress.

Act Two
Where Act One had taken place by moonlight in an
uncultivated area of the estate, this act opens in bright sunlight
on a croquet lawn with the lake still visible in the background.
It is noon on a very hot day, probably in August (although the
precise time of year is unstated). Masha, Dorn and Arkadina
are sitting around and discussing youth, age and death in an
offhand manner whilst reading aloud from a story by
Maupassant. Masha says she feels as if she is ages old.
Arkadina says she makes it a rule never to look to the future
and never to contemplate old age and death. Dorn sings to
himself, as usual, in between readings from Maupassant which
describe circumstances not unlike those pertaining between
Arkadina and Trigorin, who is offstage indulging in his
favourite pastime, fishing. Nina and Medvedenko enter,
accompanying a physically feeble Sorin. She is 'free' for three
days while her father and stepmother are away. Arkadina
quarrels with Shamrayev about the availability of carriage
horses which, he says, are needed for farm work and, in the
following scene, Polina, reacting to her husband's rude
behaviour, expresses her feelings for Dorn who, in his turn,
declares that he is too old to revive their former intimacy. Left
alone, Nina expresses naive incredulity at the ordinariness of
'famous people' who cry, fish, play cards and lose their tempers
just like average mortals. Konstantin, who has earlier been

described as being bored and listless and has rarely been seen since his play's débâcle, enters carrying a seagull which he has just shot and which he lays at Nina's feet, predicting his own self-destruction. Nina is perplexed, even irritated by the gesture, which she assumes is 'a symbol of something' (p.27).

Konstantin says that he has burned the manuscript of his play and speaks of Nina's coldness towards him, then is overcome with envy and jealousy as he sees Trigorin approaching. He quotes Hamlet's 'Words, words, words . . .' derisively and leaves. A scene follows between Nina and Trigorin in which he embarks on the lengthiest speech in all of Chekhov's major plays, describing his obsessive compulsion to write as if it were some kind of malady, a form of lunacy or addiction. Nina cannot accept this prosaic view of creativity and says, with an unconsciously ironic and prophetic air, that if she were an artist she would willingly undergo hardship and privation. Trigorin is called away to pack (Arkadina, infuriated by her estate-manager's attitude, has decided to curtail their summer break) but, before leaving, he notices the dead seagull and scribbles a few lines in his notebook, an 'idea for a short story' (p.33) in which someone like Nina will feature and who is identified, in her wanton destruction at the hands of another, with the bird. At this point, Arkadina announces from the house that they will not be leaving after all and Nina concludes the act by describing it all as 'A dream!'.

Act Three

It is one week later and the action has moved indoors to a dining room in the house. Trigorin and Arkadina are preparing to leave, the reason being Arkadina's perception of Trigorin's increasing attraction to Nina, and a challenge to a duel which Konstantin has issued to Trigorin. We also learn that Konstantin has failed in a suicide attempt brought on by a multiplicity of causes, including jealousy of Trigorin vis-à-vis both his mother and Nina, the failure of his play, plus a desperate need for attention. His problem, like Hamlet's, would seem to spring from 'neglected love'. During the opening conversation between Masha and Trigorin, she announces that

she has decided to marry Medvedenko and to tear her love for
Konstantin out of her heart 'by the roots' (p.34). Nina arrives
to say farewell to Trigorin and plays a guessing game with him
designed to resolve a decision as to whether or not to go on
the stage. He guesses incorrectly, although this appears to have
little effect on her eventual decision. Nina gives him a
medallion, engraved with Trigorin's initials plus page and line
numbers from one of his books. He hurries off to track down
the reference. Arkadina and Sorin discuss the reasons for
Konstantin's suicide attempt, which Sorin attributes to forms of
neglect, emotional and financial, before Konstantin himself
arrives and asks his mother to change the dressing on his
injured forehead. In a brief scene of tender ministration,
Konstantin reminisces about his mother's care for others before
commenting scathingly on her relationship with Trigorin and
what he construes as the latter's cowardice in evading his
challenge to a duel and lack of scruple in exploiting Nina's
emotional immaturity. The scene descends into vulgar abuse,
concluding with Arkadina's confirmation of Konstantin's worst
fears by calling him a 'Nonentity!' (p.41). This is followed by
tearful apologies and embraces of reconciliation reminiscent of
the famous 'closet scene' in *Hamlet*. Trigorin reappears, reciting
the lines referred to on the medallion, which seem to be an
invitation from Nina to make use of her life as he chooses. He
begs Arkadina to be allowed to stay another day and confesses
that he is possessed by 'sweet and marvellous dreams' of lost
youth and innocence (p.43). In response to this danger,
Arkadina acts out a melodramatic scene in a desperate attempt
to persuade him not to abandon her. Trigorin wilts under the
barrage and recognises his own form of sexual slavery and
spineless moral flabbiness. The act concludes with their
departure to catch a train for Moscow, when Arkadina
confirms her reputation for stinginess by tipping the three
servants a rouble between them. Nina has already asked to see
Trigorin before they leave and he returns to steal a final brief
meeting with her. She informs him that she has decided to run
away from home with the intention of going on the stage and
is also leaving for Moscow. He arranges to meet her there and

murmurs tender words of love, culminating in a prolonged
embrace.

Act Four

Two years have passed since the end of Act Three. The scene is
a drawing-room-cum-study in Sorin's house. It is evening and
sounds of wind and rain can be heard beyond the french
windows which lead on to an outside terrace. Masha and her
husband, Medvedenko, discuss the deterioration in Sorin's
health which has led to Arkadina's being summoned by
telegram to be at his side. Medvedenko mentions that, the
previous night, he thought he heard sounds of someone crying
coming from the skeletal fit-up stage which still stands in the
estate grounds. Trigorin will later identify it as a location for
another short story. Dorn and the ailing Sorin, now confined to
a wheelchair, talk of disappointed hopes in youth, and of
death, the doctor appearing to be rather unsympathetic to the
ailments of the old. He has just come back from Italy where
the crowded streets of Genoa had put him in mind of the
world soul of Konstantin's play. This leads to a discussion of
what has since become of Nina. It seems that she has had an
affair with Trigorin, given birth to a young son who died in
infancy and been subsequently abandoned by him in favour of
Arkadina. Konstantin describes Nina's indifferent acting career,
mentions having seen some of her poorer performances, and his
correspondence with her in which she signed herself 'Seagull'
(Chaika). It transpires that she is currently in the area, has
been barred from revisiting her home by her father and
stepmother and, for the past few days, has been living at a
local inn where she refuses to see Konstantin. Trigorin arrives,
having been fetched from the station by Arkadina. He has
brought a copy of a literary magazine containing short stories
by both himself and Konstantin. He relays some of the trivial
gossip circulating among fashionable metropolitan readers as to
the persona behind the intriguing pseudonym which Konstantin
has been adopting. The group, with the exception of Konstantin
and Medvedenko, settle down for a quick game of lotto before
dinner. Medvedenko and Masha now have a little girl, left at
home in a nanny's charge, about whom the father expresses a

maternal anxiety singularly lacking in his wife. He leaves to walk the three or so miles home in bad weather, having been denied horse transport by his father-in-law. The ensuing conversation at the lotto table ranges from Arkadina's apparently rapturous reception in Kharkov, to the deficient qualities of Konstantin's work which his mother says she has never read, to Trigorin's passion for fishing, and the fact that he has forgotten ever asking Shamrayev to have the dead seagull stuffed. The party exits to dinner leaving Konstantin alone and ruminating on the worthlessness of his own writing. He hears a knock at the french windows and goes out to reappear with a drenched and bedraggled Nina, who seems to have spent the best part of the last few days wandering the countryside like a tramp, although she claims to have horses waiting for her at the gate. She is showing distinct signs of mental distress, keeps rubbing her forehead and calling herself 'the seagull'. She breaks down in tears 'for the first time in two years' (p.62) whilst Konstantin speaks of feeling as cold as the grave. Nina seems to be semi-delirious from exhaustion and hunger (although she refuses food), loses track of what she is saying and, in the quasi-religious language of a Russian saintly wanderer, talks of endurance, having faith, bearing her cross and discovering her vocation which is, simultaneously, to be unconscious of fame or glory but also to sustain a vision of becoming 'a great actress' (pp. 64–5). She hears Trigorin's laughter from the next room and observes him through a keyhole before declaring that, despite everything, her love for him is as passionate and as desperate as ever. She says she has contracted for a winter season at a theatre in a remote provincial town and expresses fastidious distaste at the thought of having to travel in a third-class train compartment with peasants and being paid court to, albeit by a better class of local businessmen. She concludes by reciting from memory, with total accuracy, those lines from Konstantin's play which dealt with the extinction of life on earth which, she says, remind her of lost happiness and innocence. Finally, she embraces Konstantin and rushes out into the night storm. He spends the next two minutes silently tearing up all his manuscripts before exiting. The others return from the dining room intending to continue their lotto game over post-prandial drinks, and Shamrayev produces the stuffed seagull which, he says, Trigorin ordered. Trigorin tries to remember but says that he has no recollection of ever having done so. A sound like a gunshot is heard offstage. Dorn exits, reassuring an alarmed Arkadina that a phial of ether has probably burst in his medicine bag and, half a minute later, returns to confirm that this was the case, murmuring one of his songs softly to himself. Pretending to consult Trigorin about a magazine article, Dorn draws him away from the group and informs him in an undertone that Konstantin has, in fact, shot himself.

Commentary

The Seagull in context

Michael Frayn, in his Translator's Introduction, sets the play in the context of Chekhov's life and times and describes the contrasting receptions given *The Seagull* at its first performance in St Petersburg and at its second in Moscow. There is then a discussion of character and situation, the significance of the play's symbolic elements and the play-within-the-play, followed by a number of suggestive comparisons between Chekhov's own life and this play, as well as his other plays. He concludes with a discussion of the final scene of Act Four, which also raises important questions of translation. The aim of the following Commentary is to flesh out some of the themes and issues which Michael Frayn has introduced, and to place them in the broad context of European drama and artistic movements at the end of the last century.

The late nineteenth century, on the cusp of literary Modernism, was one of the most remarkable moments in the history of European drama, when a dominant Realism,[1] culminating in late-Naturalism,[2] found itself confronted by

[1] *Realism*: what constitutes reality for the artist has varied through the ages. The word derives from the Greek and 'the real', for the Greeks, was that which lay in worlds other than the immediately present one. It is only since the Renaissance that European art has tended to look at the present world as the source of what is considered to be 'real' and has been concerned with representing its external appearances accurately. A reaction against this set in with the Modernist movement at the turn of the twentieth century.

[2] *Naturalism*: Naturalism is the culmination of what Realism has come to mean in European thought and art since the Renaissance. For the out-and-out Naturalist, the only things worth taking into consideration are the observable phenomena of the material world which no longer have extra-terrestrial spiritual causation but can be observed and explained scientifically. Human beings are, in this sense, no different from animals, despite their possession of language and consciousness which, again, for the arch-materialists are physical, rather than spiritual, phenomena.

emerging forms of Symbolism[1] and Expressionism.[2] Chekhov's play may be described as an arena where these competing forms struggle for expressive dominance.

The establishment of so-called 'free' theatres in most of the major European countries provided a platform for the struggle. The Naturalist school was represented by André Antoine's 'Théâtre Libre' in France (1887), Otto Brahm's 'Freie Bühne' in Germany (1889), J.T. Grein's 'Independent Theatre' in England (1891) and the Moscow Art Theatre in Russia (1898). The Symbolist school was represented in France by Paul Fort's Théâtre d'Art (1891) and Aurélien Lugné-Poë's Théâtre de l'Oeuvre (1893) and, in Ireland, by W.B. Yeats and Lady Gregory's Abbey Theatre (1904). The Expressionist school was spearheaded by Strindberg's Intima Theatre in Sweden (1907) and was then taken up in Germany before the First World War. The major dramatists who featured in the struggle and who represented the various schools were Henrik Ibsen, August Strindberg, Gerhart Hauptmann, Maurice Maeterlinck and Anton Chekhov. Others in the background were Bernard Shaw, Lev Tolstoy, Oscar Wilde, Frank Wedekind, Alfred Jarry, Paul Claudel, W.B. Yeats and Emile Verhaeren, all of whom had plays produced during this period.

The Expressionist movement did not really make a distinctive impact on European theatre until the first two decades of the

[1] *Symbolism*: the Symbolist movement developed as a reaction against Naturalism and, in many respects, marks a return to the Greek sense of the real. Where Naturalism had purposefully dissolved distinctions between spirit and matter, mind and body, reducing a former dualistic universe to an unproblematic unity, the Symbolists headed equally purposefully in the opposite direction, suggesting that nothing in the physical word of substance and appearances had meaning except in the conceptual world of the mind.

[2] *Expressionism*: the Expressionist movement was also part of the revolt against Naturalism and tended to privilege the private world of artistic vision over the commonsensical and generally agreed perceptions of the external world. Expressionism extolled the exceptional vision of the creative individual by placing extreme importance on matters of intense idiosyncratic expression in order to deny the validity of the generally agreed and the commonplace. If the Expressionist saw the external world in distorted fragments and violent colours, then the validity of this vision was guaranteed by its special intensity.

twentieth century, although an early nineteenth-century dramatist like Georg Büchner is now seen as a forerunner, and expressionist elements are present in the dramas of Henrik Ibsen and August Strindberg, especially in *Ghosts* (1881) and *A Dream Play* (1901). Chekhov knew little, if anything, of Strindberg despite being given a Russian translation of *The Father* in 1899 and despite being heralded, in 1897, as representing 'a mighty, mysterious miracle of Strindberg content in Maupassant form' (Rayfield: 1997, p.443). He did know something about Ibsen's plays, which he didn't much like, and was very interested in the on-going debates between the Naturalists and the Symbolists and was an admirer of the work of the Belgian Symbolist dramatist, Maurice Maeterlinck.

Chekhov was also an admirer of Darwin and was familiar with theories of evolution and determinism. Without ever being as crudely reductionist as the neo-Darwinians, he seems to have shared their down-to-earth, common-sense explanation of phenomena and believed in a 'scientific' attitude to the world which, minus its Marxist political coloration, anticipates that of Bertolt Brecht. 'Heredity' and 'environment', key watchwords in the naturalist approach to deterministic factors at work in the conditioning of human behaviour, as stated in Zola's preface to his novel *Thérèse Raquin* (1867) and by Strindberg in his preface to *Miss Julie* (1888), are clearly apparent in the world of *The Seagull*. In many respects Konstantin is someone who is destroyed by his environment and who can never become the artist he wishes to be because, like Hamlet, he is 'too much i' the sun [son]'. In other words, before he is a writer, Konstantin is portrayed, first and foremost, as a son paralysed into creative immobility by thoughts of his inferior social status (derived from his 'shopkeeper' father) and psychologically wrecked by emotional dependence on his mother. Another influential figure lurking in the background to this play is, of course, Freud who developed the theory of the 'Oedipus complex' and whose first paper on infantile sexuality was published in 1898. In these terms, virtually all the characters in *The Seagull* can be seen as frustrated victims of circumstances, guilty of little other than having been born to these parents under these conditions. However, as Raymond Williams noted in his statements about

Naturalism, to reproduce exactly an environment on stage is itself a kind of physical trap, confirming the naturalist philosophy which stresses the determining effects of genetic inheritance and environmental influence, as well as the primacy of instinctual response over reasoned behaviour. (See Raymond Williams, 'The Case of English Naturalism' in M. Axton & R. Williams (eds), *English Drama: Forms and Development* (Cambridge: CUP, 1977), pp.203–24.)

That Chekhov was aware of the limitations of a naturalist view when applied to the world seems clear from his interest in those art forms which seemed to offer an idealistic alternative, especially in the shape of the Symbolist movement whose prioritising of 'other worlds' than the materialist seems a direct response to the fearful recognition of naturalist entrapment. It is important to establish Chekhov's attitude to the Russian Symbolists as it directly affects the significance of Konstantin's play-within-the-play. Recent Russian research has revealed the extent to which, despite its naturalist trappings, *The Seagull* owes a considerable debt to the emerging world of Russian Symbolism, with its poetic and philosophic dimensions. The first edition of the almanac *Russian Symbolists*, edited by the poet Valeri Briusov, appeared in February 1894, the year in which Chekhov was completing work on *The Seagull*. A play by Briusov, *Passions of Estate Life (Dachnye strasti)*, written in 1893 had been banned but had dealt, in parodic form, with the relations between a 'new poet', Findes'eklev (a pun on 'fin-de-siècle'), and his stifling environment. Between 1892 and 1895 the poet, novelist and Symbolist theorist, Dmitri Merezhkovskii, published his *Symbols (Songs and Poems)*, whilst the Symbolist philosopher, Vladimir Solov'ev, published his own poems at a time when translations of poems by the French Symbolist, Baudelaire, had appeared, in 1895.

Chekhov was known to have been enthusiastic about the poetry of Konstantin Bal'mont, whose volume of verse *Beneath Northern Skies (Pod severnym nebom)* appeared in 1894, a copy of which was given to Chekhov by Bal'mont himself. The sequence contains a poem called 'The Seagull' (Chaika) which, in rough translation, reads as follows:

Gull, grey gull who with sad cries traverses
The cold abyss of the sea
Whither do you hasten? Wherefore? Why her complaints
So full of boundless suffering?

Endless space. The uninviting heavens frown
The foam furls grey on the wave crests
The north wind weeps and the seagull sobs, mad
Shelterless seagull from a distant land.

A play by Dmitri Merezhkovskii, *Proshla groza* (The Storm
Has Passed), appeared in 1893, about which Chekhov wrote to
his friend, the publisher Suvorin, and in which Merezhkovskii
satirises French Naturalist writers (of whom Trigorin in *The
Seagull* may be said to be an epigone). The play's hero is a
sculptor and a member of the 'Decadents'[1] (to which group
Arkadina dismissively assigns Konstantin's play), obsessed with
death and with his love for one Elena, and who, finally,
commits suicide. Critics suggested that Merezhkovskii had been
influenced by the artistic theories of Max Nordau,[2] who
associated late-nineteenth-century art with aestheticism and
amorality, psychic illness and lack of will. Chekhov was
familiar with Max Nordau's influential work *Degeneration* and,
after the first performance of *The Seagull*, critics noted
'decadent' influences, not only in Konstantin's play but in
Chekhov's play as a whole. One S. Ia. Ukolov even wrote a
parody of the play in which Treplev asked, at one point, what
would become of Komissarzhevskaya's soul in 200,000 years'
time [Komissarzhevskaya acted the role of Nina in the first

[1] The so-called Decadent movement in Russia both pre-dated and succeeded
the Symbolist movement with which it had much in common, but which was
characterised by a greater concern with aestheticism, sensationalism and religious perverseness.

[2] *Max Nordau* (1849–1923): a Hungarian theorist who was taken to task by
Bernard Shaw in his essay 'The Sanity of Art' for his aesthetic views. Nordau
dedicated his own book, *Degeneration* (1895), to an Italian professor of
psychiatry who believed that heredity determines character, that there are born
criminal types and that degenerates can pass as great artists but should be
exposed for what they are. Nordau denounced practically all nineteenth-century
art and literature as manifestations of a degenerate civilisation.

production]. The satire was called *The Seagull: Fantastically-mad Scenes with a Prologue, Epilogue, Balderdash and Flop (the topic borrowed from a hospital for the mentally insane).*

The interest of Chekhov's play may be seen in the extent to which he incorporates both naturalist and symbolist perspectives within his work, forging his drama out of the conflict between them without, finally, conceding victory in the struggle to either tendency.

The seagull and the enchanted lake

The way in which the image of the seagull and the lake are deployed within the play are crucially relevant to the question of naturalist and symbolist interpretations. When asked by the actor who played Trigorin in the 1905 revival of *The Seagull* what he had to say about the significance of the lake, Chekhov is purported to have replied, 'Well, it's wet . . .'. For most of the characters in the play the lake has romantic and magical associations. For Konstantin it is the only suitable background for a play in which Nature has survived the extinction of humanity; for Dorn it is the source of the witchcraft of love which appears to affect the young people in the drama; for Arkadina it memorialises her youth, love, song, and evenings of revelry; for Nina it seems to exude a captivating charm by which she feels drawn, as if in a fairy tale where she sees herself transformed into a seagull soaring above its surface. On the other hand, for Trigorin it is a place to go fishing and for the estate workers somewhere to wash and swim in.

In other words, the lake is never a neutral phenomenon but derives its meaning from human use and attribution. Its essential 'lakeness' can only exist when all human life has been extinguished from the earth and there is nobody left to describe it in words. During Chekhov's lifetime, lakes had a habit of being endowed with romantic and mystical properties and one of his greatest admirers was the composer Tchaikovsky, whose admiration Chekhov reciprocated, and whose ballet *Swan Lake* epitomises the fairy-tale enchantment, as well as the dangers which magic lakes of this order possess. In one version of the ballet, a swan is killed by a hunter with a cross-bow, much as the seagull is shot down by Konstantin. It is perhaps symptomatic that another Russian composer, Anatoli Lyadov, also wrote a work called *The Enchanted Lake* (in 1909).

Effectively, the lake has a number of 'meanings' attributed to it by the various characters and none is more valid than any other. The same is true of the seagull. Much has been made of the connection with Ibsen's *The Wild Duck*, in which a young pubescent girl appears to learn the language of symbolic meaning to the extent that she identifies herself with an already injured wild duck, decides to sacrifice it to appease her father but ends up by shooting herself, either accidentally or on purpose. Chekhov, apart from declaring that Ibsen was no dramatist, is also on record as saying that *The Wild Duck* was his favourite play, although doubtless he was being ironic at the time. However, this does not rule out the validity of comparing the symbolic meaning of the duck with that of the seagull, where Ibsen and Chekhov appear to be on the same wavelength. As Donald Rayfield has pointed out, 'the symbol of the seagull belongs not to the author but to the impoverished imagination of his characters' (Rayfield: 1999, p.141). In other words, both Ibsen and Chekhov seem concerned with the potentially dangerous tendency to attribute significance to the external world as an aspect of a claim to *personal* significance. The world and the objects in it only have meaning in so far as the individual is prepared to accord them such. This may be creatively necessary for the genuine poet (as well as being the source of the 'pathetic fallacy') but it can be a disastrously mistaken activity for the less-gifted and self-conceited. As well as being the activity of the poet it is also the activity of the paranoid and insane.

It is fairly certain that when the main characters in the play think of a seagull, they imagine something beautiful, and in flight symbolising aspiration and freedom in association with the sky. When we imagine Konstantin shooting the seagull, it has to be out of the sky, not whilst settled on the surface of the lake with its wings folded, like a kind of 'sitting duck'. When Nina thinks of herself as a seagull in Act One it is clearly as the 'in flight' version; her later identification (or denial of identification) is with something which has been shot down, or 'winged'. Significantly, nobody in the play conceives of the seagull as a scavenger with a razor-sharp bill and a raucous cry, drawn to fish and rubbish heaps and which, when walking rather than in flight, can seem both ugly and absurd. The *characters* seem incapable of conceiving this but Chekhov and the play seem very aware of this naturalistic perspective which is opposed to the largely symbolic one.

Both versions of the seagull offered above are imaginative constructions. Neither 'appear' in the play and the 'down-to-earth' variants have been 'construed' in dialectical opposition to the aerial. They are 'intellectual' versions of the bird. Noticeably, the only versions which can actually be made manifest in the physical world of the play, where naturalist and symbolist versions compete for attention, are a dead seagull, on the one hand, and its inanimate, seemingly living, resurrected correlate on the other. The stuffed seagull is, in its own way, a work of art in being a realistic representation of something once alive. But here the 'artist' who produced the stuffed seagull is a taxidermist and the impression of life is a false one. The play would seem to be establishing playfully serious analogies between naturalistic forms of dramatic representation and taxidermy, with the implication that 'realistic' representations of everyday life cannot get beyond the impression of a world of 'stuffed dummies' or 'mannequins'.

To the Naturalists, the same laws of environment and heredity apply at every social level and any inequalities are therefore culturally created and not scientifically justified. As Chekhov famously observed in another context, dungheaps have just as respectable a place in a landscape as flowerbeds. However, the play seems to be aware of the danger of eroding distinctions between one thing and another – between seagulls and people (whether living or stuffed), between suicide and bursting bottles of ether, between beggars and those who are housed and clothed. The actress playing Nina in Act Four, when havering between her identity as 'seagull' or 'actress', perhaps needs to ask herself whether Nina knows what a seagull is and, if she does not, whether she has any idea what an actress is either?

A corollary of the erosion of distinctions between flowerbeds and dungheaps is that we may believe we live in a world of flowers (a leitmotif of the play) but we actually live in a dungheap. A point which then relates to the seagull is, that if you lose sight of its 'down-to-earth' meanings and associate solely with its 'higher' imaginative manifestations, then the fact that its habitat is often rubbish heaps gets overlooked.

Another thing about the seagull is its relation to Bal'mont's poem, the storm in Act Four and Nina as a 'homeless wanderer'. The site of the Sorin estate is never specified but it seems fair to guess that it is far inland and represents an unlikely haunt for seagulls. The point Chekhov would seem to be making is that this does not really matter but if you want a 'realistic' explanation of how a seagull comes to be so far inland it is because it has been blown there by a very severe storm. However, that explanation is itself 'symbolic' of a general human condition where one half of a binary opposition is being ignored or suppressed. In a dualistic world, 'calm' is necessarily in tandem with 'storm', and to the extent that characters in the play tend to suppress a recognition of 'storm' in favour of 'calm', the other (like the Freudian 'return of the repressed') asserts its reality with commensurate force – literally so in Act Four. Perhaps only Nina and Konstantin discover that 'calm' is an illusion. But to move from one extreme to the other does not necessarily guarantee the 'truth' of its opposite and Nina's actual condition seems to be one of unstable oscillation between categories – calm and storm, natural creature and human actress, sanity and madness. The others merely ossify (or mummify), Dorn's final response to disaster being absurdly, and calmly, typical. Konstantin resolves the problem of unstable binary oppositions by destroying their mental source. We have to imagine that, like Hedda Gabler in Ibsen's play, he shoots himself in the head rather than through the heart.

The play-within-the-play

Probably the first thing to note about Konstantin's play is that it is a polemical riposte to the kind of theatre he has criticised in conversation with his uncle early in Act One. What he has been describing is a typical naturalistic play of the mid-to late-nineteenth century which presented 'a slice of life' in which people go about their everyday affairs in an apparently undramatic way. It is the kind of theatre which Chekhov himself seemed to espouse when he wrote: 'Things on stage should be as complicated and yet as simple as in life. People dine, just dine, while their happiness is made and their lives are smashed.' If one thinks of the last act of *The Seagull*, this would seem to describe Chekhov's play perfectly.

Konstantin's play attempts to take drama out of the theatre and return it to its place in the natural world, and it is certainly the case that the history of professional Russian theatre follows the pattern of Western theatre after 1700 in confining play production to enclosed buildings. Forms of popular entertainment continued to be staged in the open air, however. Konstantin's practice is, in essence, closer to the Greeks, the Romans and the Elizabethans in having his theatre open to the elements, even if its form, with a wooden proscenium arch and a drop curtain, retains the lineaments of late-nineteenth-century naturalistic staging. In this sense, the requirement that there be 'scenery' and that the scenery be 'natural' can be seen as a contradiction in terms. It was the introduction of perspective setting in the early seventeenth century which introduced the idea of 'scenery' into the theatre – a post-Renaissance phenomenon and one which was alien to the Greeks, the Romans and the Elizabethans. Konstantin's theatre appears to embrace a return to the form of the Greek amphitheatre – open to the skies and set in a natural landscape – whilst retaining the scenic conventions of post-Renaissance realism. In an actual performance of *The Seagull*, the ironies of these conflicting demands are immediately apparent in so far as the 'real' setting of Konstantin's play is necessarily as artificial as the play in which Konstantin and the others are being dramatised by Chekhov. The interesting question then becomes, to what extent does Chekhov's play differ from Konstantin's?

At the heart of Konstantin's play, even in its truncated form, is a debate which had been exercising Russian thinkers and artists throughout the nineteenth century and which was to culminate in the Russian Revolution of 1917. This was a debate between the materialists and the idealists. On the one hand were those who considered the spiritual world a fiction, that religion was the opiate of the people and that scientific and economic explanations of phenomena were the only significant ones. On the other hand were the idealists and religious philosophers who, in the footsteps of Plato, considered the material world to be merely a shadow of some other, ideal world elsewhere. Among the key figures in the debate were Chernyshevskii[1] and Lenin on the materialist side and Dostoevsky and Vladimir Solov'ev (pronounced Soloviov) on the religio-idealistic wing. Solov'ev (1853–1900) was the most important metaphysical thinker behind the Russian Symbolist movement and his ideas are central to Konstantin's play. It is also worth noting that the contrasts in Chekhov's play between ideal and material versions of the world characterise Solov'ev's own spiritual development, as he veered between religious and secular modes of thought before settling on an evolutionary vision of the world which incorporated both in total harmony – a future moment which Konstantin's play anticipates when all human life has disappeared.

According to Solov'ev, 'Through a free act of the World-Soul, the world which it animates fell away from God and broke up into a number of hostile elements; through a long series of free acts the rebellious multitude must be reconciled to itself and to God, becoming regenerated in the form of an absolute organism' (N.O. Lossky, *History of Russian Philosophy* (London: Allen and Unwin, 1952), p.102). Even in a world that has fallen away from God, meaning is preserved in

---

[1] *Chernyshevskii*: Nikolai Chernyshevskii (1828-89) was a crucial figure in nineteenth-century Russian thought whose essay *The Aesthetic Relations of Art to Reality* (1855) claimed that science was more important than art and that the common people were the true arbiters of artistic taste and beauty. Chernyshev-skii was strongly influenced by German materialist philosophy and considered the mind/body dichotomy a non-problem when seen from a scientifically rational point of view. He saw the doctrine of enlightened self-interest, when rationally contemplated, as informing all human affairs and set out his philosophical programme in a novel *What is to be Done?* (1863). This was ridiculed by Dostoevsky in his *Notes from Underground* (1864) but was seized on by Lenin as an example of best practice which he celebrated in his own non-fictional *What is to be Done?* (1902).

so far as all beings have a vague instinctive longing for an all-embracing unity; this transcends the limits of each separate person and, as the universal inner life of all that exists, may be called the World-Soul. The point which Konstantin makes in his play about the atomic structure of animate and inanimate forms and the state of constant flux also finds its parallel in Solov'ev's thought, for whom, 'It is not energy which is the attribute of matter, as must be supposed by mechanistic materialism, but on the contrary, matter is only the result of energies, or more correctly speaking, the general limit of their interaction'. The atoms are 'immaterial dynamic entities existing in themselves, they are *living energies or monads* existing in themselves and acting out of themselves' (ibid., p.100, italics in original).

Chekhov's characters may be said to be precisely of this order – self-enclosed monads who exist in themselves and who act out of themselves. What Konstantin's play, and by implication Chekhov himself, is suggesting, is that the characters do not imagine themselves to be *immaterial*. They believe they exist in the fullest possible individual sense, their confidence in this deriving from a belief in the significance of a material world which is actually only a shadow of the real thing. Konstantin's play insists, albeit naively, that we are spirit rather than matter and the fact that we behave as if the opposite were true means that the external world we inhabit as if it were replete and meaningful is, in fact, an empty void like our inner sense of personal identity. The void, in this sense, is 'the self' with its appetites and priorities.

A crucial point of dramatic interpretation in any performance of *The Seagull* is how the production decides to interpret Konstantin's play. Is it a ludicrously deficient attempt at a symbolist play and thus a satire on Konstantin's pretensions and the ethos of the Russian Symbolists? Is it a naive but brave attempt to break away from naturalist conventions by way of experimentation in a valid new form? Or does the very fact of *performance* get in the way of any artistic claims the play may or may not have on our attention? The play is not *Hamlet* but no matter how fine a play we might acknowledge *Hamlet* to be, poor acting and a bad production can make it seem like a

nightmare. How much the worse, then, for a work without an
established reputation whose merits, at a first performance, are
intrinsically bound up with acting and production? The
circumstances and the reception of Konstantin's play sound very
much like the first night of *The Seagull*, in fact (see Translator's
Introduction, p. lxxx). In this sense it is important to note that
the play is staged by amateurs, some of whom have knowledge
of the theatre, some of whom have none whatsoever.
Interestingly, it is at the point where those, like Yakov,
intervene who have no knowledge of theatre that the play in
production is seen to collapse. Why? Because the participants
have not been rehearsed sufficiently. Why haven't they been
rehearsed? Because they are regarded as peasants with no
understanding of the theatre, their capacity lying in an ability
to obey instructions and merely construct the shell of the
material stage into which the spiritual art they do not
comprehend will be poured.

It is no accident that Chekhov opens the play with invisible
peasants but with the sounds and visible results of their labour
– the improvised stage on which Konstantin's fate is to be
decided. It also becomes clear that Yakov, at least, has been
cast in the play as the Devil but it is not clear that his role has
been rehearsed, especially as he has no words to say. The only
evidence that Nina has actually rehearsed the play lies in the
fact that she has learned the lines, but the extent to which she
personally, or the play as a whole, has been rehearsed remains
unclear. Konstantin clearly prioritises the intellectual and
symbolic significance of his work and does not seem especially
concerned with the means of production or with utilitarian
matters, even where these impinge on performance and
interpretation. At the same time, as someone interested in
matters of eternity, he seems ludicrously preoccupied with clock
time, even imposing its mechanical rigidities on the natural
world. Moons do not rise at any particular time in an eternal
world of Nature, but this one has to rise at 8.30 when
measured by human chronological norms.

Chekhov's play constantly emphasises Konstantin's place in
both the material and spiritual worlds and he is shown to
neglect the material world at his peril. It is at the point where

Yakov clumsily intervenes as the Father of Eternal Matter, that the credibility of the play breaks down, not because of its intrinsic demerits as a play, but because a peasant has been casually drafted in to a crucial role which he does not understand and whose actions have clearly been under-rehearsed. The moment also gives rise to Arkadina's offended sense of comic outrage, less at the play, one imagines, than at the sight of an estate worker playing a role in one. It is *her* profession which is at stake. The moment also provides the opportunity she has been waiting for to lash out at something which she doesn't understand and may feel intimidated by. She is aided and abetted in this by the self-destructive talents of Konstantin himself who, at this crucial moment, finds his own situation vis-à-vis his mother more dramatically involving than his role as a playwright with something important to say. Characteristically, he is neglectful of the effect on Nina of his truncating the performance so abruptly and apparently unaware of the reactions to his play of anyone other than his mother. It becomes clear, for example, that both Medvedenko and Dorn were absorbed by it, as was Trigorin. But their responses seem to count for nothing in Konstantin's eyes.

Time and memory; youth and age; sleep and dream

A useful service performed by Konstantin's play is in its handling of the concept of Time. Without being a religious play, it introduces the idea of Eternity, or at least aeons of time in which the characters will have ceased to exist. The time of their non-existence, within a span of 200,000 years, ought to be a salutary reference point for defining what their existence means in terms of day-to-day activity. To what extent does non-existence colour existence – even erode it altogether?

Characters in *The Seagull* are constantly preoccupied with time present and time past but, apart from Konstantin, seem little concerned with time future. At the beginning of Act One, Konstantin is simultaneously preoccupied with eternity (in his play) and with clock time at the moment of performance (he is constantly consulting his watch in concern at the moon's imminent appearance and Nina's, late, non-appearance).

Arkadina is preoccupied with the past, with her age – with seeming to be fifteen when she is forty-five, with what life used to be like on the estate in summers past. She says she is not prepared to think about old age and death. Sorin, who has spent 'twenty-eight years in the department' and longs 'to live', is a visible symbol of physical fragility as he enacts, during the course of the play, the stages of Oedipus' answer to the riddle of the Sphinx (see p.80 in Notes), even passing beyond 'three legs' to four wheels, and seems to think that a joke about spending the night 'on his back' means sleep rather than death.

Masha seems old before her time, and speaks of being born 'a long, long time ago'. She is 'in mourning' for her life which, whilst an obvious pose at one level, becomes a philosophical deathwish almost by default. Polina wishes to rekindle past passions by seeking to arouse a previous relationship with Dorn, but he reacts as if, at the age of fifty-five, his active life is over as both lover and obstetrician. He recalls once being a decent doctor 'ten years ago'. Now, all he can do is prescribe valerian drops. 'Time's running out for us, we're not young any more,' declares Polina, but all she has in mind is her own predicament without fully realising the implications of what she is saying. 'We mustn't waste time,' she declares, whilst settling down to a game of lotto prior to yet another meal. Shamrayev is fixated on the past – specific years, past performers – whom Arkadina describes, significantly, as 'out of the Ark' ('antedeluvian' in the original) or indulges memories of an amateur church chorister who outdid a professional in profundity of sound.

Arkadina can memorise the poetry of Nekrasov, can recall two ballet dancers, but apparently forgets ever having been kind to a washerwoman. She asks to be remembered kindly by others but then forgets the parting gift of plums Polina has brought. She recalls summer evenings by the lake and the lotto game they used to play as children with their mother and her final action is to remember, with rapidly suppressed horror, Konstantin's attempted suicide without seeming to have thought about its significance in the meantime. In spite of her reservations about Konstantin's play in Act One, Nina still remembers it through the intervening years and recites it

faultlessly in Act Four. Trigorin, by contrast, has a total
memory lapse when it comes to the stuffed seagull, having told
Nina, a week after the performance, how he will always
remember her as she was when she appeared on the stage. In
Act Four he refreshes his memories of two years past by
revisiting the site of the abandoned improvised stage. However,
he shows no effects of what has supposedly passed between
himself and Nina during the same period. Act Four, in fact,
seems almost entirely preoccupied with time and memory and
death. Sorin is now ill; Dorn considers the fear of death to be
'an animal fear'. The characters recall the past, now in the
changed circumstances of storm and tempest, with the
improvised stage a skeletal reminder of the ravages of time, its
existence offstage constantly referred to as past and present
seem to merge into one. 'We're all getting a little weather-
beaten,' Shamrayev suggests.

One of the reviews of the first production of *The Seagull*
described the actors as dazed sleepwalkers. This was intended
to imply that they did not understand the play, had a shaky
grasp of their lines, and appeared to wander inconsequentially
about the stage. In fact, the reviewer appears to have grasped
an essential feature of a play in which, when characters are not
actually sleeping, or sitting idly, they are all, to a greater or
lesser degree, in a trance or dream-like state. There are three
words which the play deploys fairly consistently – 'son',
'mechta' and 'greza' (pronounced 'grioza') – all implying states
of dreaminess in which the unsatisfactoriness of present
physical and material circumstances is rendered bearable by
mental escape into daydream, sleep, or a vision of a future in
which circumstances have changed the material world into an
ideal one.

Sorin's life is like 'a bad dream' in which he has not lived
the life he wished to and contemplates his epitaph as 'The Man
Who Wished . . .'; for Konstantin, Nina is 'my enchantress, my
dream'. She describes his play as devoid of living characters but
it seeks to show life 'as it is in dreams' and asks that the
audience 'dream' of life in a future in which 'non-existence' will
be shown, to which Arkadina replies 'We're fast asleep', as if
she genuinely thinks herself 'awake'. Nina 'dreams' of going on

the stage; Dorn even dreams of being a creative artist and
scorning 'this material envelope of mine'. Even Masha's foot
'goes to sleep'. Nina 'dreams' of triumph and glory where she
both has her chariot dragged through the streets in triumph and
lives in a garret on black bread. Her comment at the end of
Act Two is that it's all 'a dream'. Trigorin, the writer of
realistic prose who, like Sorin, also contemplates his epitaph at
one point, suddenly metamorphoses into a dreamer in Act
Three and asks to be borne off 'into the land of dreams'.
Finally, Konstantin announces that he is still 'floundering in a
chaos of dreams', as if others had awoken and were not just
sleepwalkers going through the motions of living a life.

Art and life; love and destruction

One way of escaping the circumstances of life is to retreat into
the realm of literature and art. This is something that
characters in *The Seagull* seem adept at doing. The play is full
of references to artists and works of art into which all of the
characters seem to project themselves in fantasy.

Characters seem only too ready to allow themselves to be
used as artistic subjects, or objects. 'If ever you have need of
my life, then come and take it,' says Nina to Trigorin, with the
implication that she consents to being used both in life and in a
fiction. If she does not succeed in becoming an actress, at least
she will feature in a short story where her fictional existence is
seen to be more significant than her factual one. Masha
dramatises the hopelessness of her love for Konstantin in a
manner which suggests that, were it to be requited, she would
lose her reason for living, which is to act out the role of
unrequited lover in the theatre of her own mind. She is
melodramatically 'in mourning' for her life or 'resident in the
world for reasons unknown', and at the beginning of Act
Three, seems to be offering Konstantin's suicide attempt to
Trigorin as a subject for a short story. As someone who 'takes
snuff' and is married to a school teacher, she has already been
identified by Trigorin as fictional subject matter. She may even
be seen to regard her own 'dubious descent' as fictional
material of a quasi-romantic order. In fact, in the first version

of the play, the fact that her father could be Dorn rather than Shamrayev was more clearly signposted (see Translator's Introduction, p.lxxxvi).

Both Arkadina and Konstantin inhabit the realms of art – the one romantic melodrama, the other the world of symbolist fantasy. Interestingly, they see their own mother and son relationship in terms of an art work, not only quoting from *Hamlet* and alluding to the play at several points, but also acting out some of its scenes, such as 'the closet scene', where Konstantin berates Arkadina for her affair with Trigorin much in the manner of Hamlet berating Gertrude for her marriage to Claudius. Arkadina never ceases to be 'on stage', her overweening egotism perhaps compensating for the fact that she appears once to have been a performer on the Imperial stage and no amount of provincial plaudits can make up for a sense of theatrical downgrading. A good reception in Kharkov is not the same as one in Moscow or St Petersburg.

Even Medvedenko seeks to have his life as a teacher fictionally commemorated when he invites Trigorin to consider the plight of the teaching profession when it comes to a choice of literary topic. Dorn appears to live in a self-absorbed world of operatic and popular song, which not only suggests he was a frequenter of theatres and opera houses in the past but also that he now seeks comfort in snatches of song to avoid confronting difficult experience. Even whilst walking in a Genoese crowd he says he is put in mind of a work of art – Konstantin's play. Shamrayev is an estate-manager but his imaginative world seems populated almost entirely by artists and singers of the past. In conversation with others, he seems to wish to establish himself as a knowledgeable critic of both acting and singing instead of something rather more down-to-earth and practical. This might well be one of the reasons why the estate does not seem to be especially well-managed. His mind is on higher things than husbandry and carriage maintenance.

Nina's entry in the play seems to be straight out of the worlds of fairy tale and romantic melodrama, as she arrives on horseback having galloped apace in a race against the setting sun. Like a princess, she is fleeing from the equivalent of a castle tower in which she has been imprisoned by her wicked stepmother and brutal father, and under whose window Konstantin sees himself holding vigil like a lovelorn troubadour or knight-at-arms. The land of Bohemia with which Nina identifies is one populated by famous people and 'great' writers who are great by reason of being famous. Nina's impatience with Konstantin's play and with its author is partly because neither chimes with her idea of what a play is or what a writer should be. Her fantasy world includes her own fame and glory as an actress but she gives no indication of having read any serious plays or of knowing what it means to act on a stage. By Act Four, an audience may be convinced that she has acquired the kind of life experience which might equip her for performance in tragedy, but does Nina's concept of stage performance include comedy, or even farce?

Critics have frequently noted that *The Seagull* depicts a succession of frustrated and unrequited love relationships where A is in love with B who is in love with C, etc. What also needs to be indicated is the extent to which love and destruction are intimately related in the play. It is symptomatic that Konstantin's illustration of his mother's love for him involves tearing petals off a flower, just as Polina's love for Dorn and jealousy of Nina is expressed by her destruction of a nosegay of flowers. Masha's love for Konstantin has destructive consequences in so far as she opts deliberately for a loveless marriage to Medvedenko and appears to neglect their child as a thoughtless consequence. Again, her decision not to love Konstantin is expressed in terms of the destruction of nature, something which will be torn out 'by the roots', just as Konstantin's love for Nina finds expression in the destruction of the seagull. Love between mother and son is shown to be both destructive and self-destructive, as Konstantin destroys first his play and then himself. In this he is prompted first by Arkadina's rejection of his work, then by Nina's rejection of both his work and his love. Trigorin's love for Nina and hers for him is patently destructive of both Nina and her child, although we never learn why or how the child dies. Whether Nina herself is suicidal at the end remains, possibly, a moot point. She is associated with the lake and has associations with

Ophelia as well as Pushkin's *Rusalka* (see A Note on the
Translation, p.xciv). When audiences were questioned at the
Moscow Art Theatre in 1898 as to what they thought became
of Nina at the end, apparently most in the stalls said she
became a provincial actress whilst those in the gallery said she
probably threw herself in the lake.

Comedy or tragedy?

How can a play in which the youthful male lead commits
suicide at the end be called a comedy? This puzzled Chekhov's
interpreters at the time, Stanislavsky insisting in face of the
author's denial, that the plays which Chekhov designated
comedies were, in fact, tragedies. However, just as it can be
argued that, with the demise of the world of Ancient Greece,
tragedy ceased to be a pure genre, most attempts to retain the
genres of tragedy and comedy in separate compartments have
since failed, the most successful works of tragedy (such as those
of Shakespeare) consisting of a mixture of both genres. French
neo-classical tragedy and comedy of the seventeenth century
was probably the last successful attempt to keep the genres
apart, although Molière's comedy may be seen to teeter on the
brink of tragedy.

There were examples of neo-classical tragedy in Russian
dramatic literature of the late-eighteenth and nineteenth
centuries, although the most significant tragedy of nineteenth-
century Russia, Pushkin's *Boris Godunov*, is Shakespearean in
the way it mixes the genres. There were also tragedies of
peasant life and of the Russian merchant class written by
nineteenth-century Russian dramatists such as Aleksei Pisemsky,
Lev Tolstoy and Aleksandr Ostrovsky but which, according to
classical and neo-classical definitions of tragedy, in not being
concerned with people of 'high estate', negated their status as
works with universal tragic implications. However, the point
that needs to be made is that the greatest Russian dramas have
tended to be comedies rather than tragedies, and this is as true
of the twentieth century as of the nineteenth. The tradition that
Chekhov belongs to is more that of Gogol and Turgenev, in a
Russian context, and that of Ibsen and (later) Beckett in a

broader European context.

The effect of the Naturalist movement on both Ibsen and Chekhov lay not only in the realistically representational forms of theatrical staging it demanded, but also in the depiction of the lives of ordinary people which naturalist thought established as viable dramatic subject matter. However, what Ibsen discovered was that the very ordinariness of ordinary lives did not lend itself easily to dignified and tragic elevation. Naturalist philosophy was egalitarian. If the laws of heredity and environment applied to everyone, then any distinctions were socially, rather than existentially, determined. If universal laws are not metaphysical ones but simply scientific, biological, physiological and environmental then, not only can there be no denying them, but the attempt to challenge them can no longer be represented as aspirationally God-like, but merely pointless and absurd, like banging one's head against a brick wall. If all that can be said, with any degree of scientific, biological validity, is that Man is related to the animals rather than to the angels, then that which makes human beings different from animals – language and consciousness – are merely freakish, evolutionary attributes of no particular significance.

The Naturalists seemed quite content with this version of the world, apparently given sanction by Darwin and others, whilst the Symbolists were desperately unhappy with it, recognising the truth of its perceptions but also the need to redefine and recreate the realm of the spiritual in a new religious sense. It is at this point of 'impasse' that Chekhov composed *The Seagull*, when it seemed that nothing was clear, especially generic distinctions between the tragic and the comic. The theme of the play then becomes this disjunction of realms where those on stage seem to be behaving according to norms which no longer apply or can no longer be taken for granted.

The genre to which *The Seagull* may be said to belong is 'tragi-comedy', where a suicidal gunshot is greeted in a manner of almost complete inconsequence, as if what has happened offstage is an unfortunate mishap – as significant as the explosion of a bottle of ether. A death has become the equivalent of a yawn. In these terms the 'tragedy' lies as much in Nina's survival as in Konstantin's suicide. They have both sought to redeem this fallen world through art – he as a playwright, she as an actress. It is therefore ironic that Nina's performance of part of Konstantin's play in Act Four should serve to establish his play's genuine dramatic credentials whilst simultaneously precipitating Konstantin's suicide. Neither recognises its significance as a work of art, both being over-preoccupied with their individual claims for recognition. Nina survives to pursue the claims of a serious dramatic art which once had spiritual grandeur and dignity when it stood for a *collective* tragic sense, but which has now become, in the world of nineteenth-century theatre, merely a vehicle for individual, melodramatic and meaningless posturing. In other words, Konstantin's first-act critique of nineteenth-century theatre is revealed to be perfectly valid and *The Seagull* can be seen as a work which goes some way towards answering Konstantin's call for 'new forms'.

Problems of translation

Some problems in the translation of Chekhov, and of this play in particular, will be referred to in the Notes at the end and are also the subject of an essay by Richard Peace (in Miles: 1993, pp.216–25). Tom Stoppard also has some interesting things to say about problems of translating *The Seagull* when you have no Russian and are dependent on so-called 'literal' versions (see his introduction to *The Seagull*, Faber and Faber, 1997). Translation is always a matter of interpretation and it may be worthwhile focusing on three moments in the play where translation seems clearly a matter of how the translator interprets the play as a whole.

Towards the end of Act One, following the moment where Dorn takes the snuffbox from Masha and flings it away (p.19), he says, after a pause: 'V dome, kazhetsia, igraiut. Nado idti', which literally translates as 'In the house, it seems, they're playing. Must go,' or more idiomatically, 'They're playing in the house it seems. I'd better go [i.e. and join them].' Most translations and productions assume that Dorn hears music at this point: 'They seem to be having music up at the house' (Calderon); 'They're playing the piano indoors' (Magarshack);

'Someone's playing the piano' (Cook); 'They seem to be playing
there in the house' (Dunnigan); 'I think someone's playing the
piano indoors' (Hingley); 'I fancy I hear music in the house'
(Koteliansky); 'I can hear someone playing' (Alexander);
'Somebody's playing the piano' (Schmidt); 'There's music at the
house' (van Itallie); 'It seems there's music in the house'
(Bristow). Significant exceptions to this general rule are the
version by Tom Stoppard, from a 'literal' by Joanna Wright,
who has: 'They'll be playing cards now,' and the present
translation's 'I think they've starting playing cards inside'. The
only one who translates what is on the page is Ann Dunnigan;
all the others make assumptions about the kind of world these
characters inhabit – most are romantically associated with
music; two conceive a more commonplace activity, possibly
prompted by the game of lotto in Act Four.

No translator appears to have taken on board the fact that
this is a play about actors and the theatre and that the verb
'igrat' in Russian means, as it does in English, both 'to play'
and 'to act'. The characters in the house could be engaged in a
number of things – they could be playing instruments, either
individually or collectively or listening to others do so; they
could be playing card or board games; they could be playing
other kinds of game, or they could be acting out roles in a
game of charades. The point perhaps lies in a deliberate lack of
definition but where the verb 'to play' takes on all these
possibilities it certainly ought to include the possibility of
being a player on a stage.

Another case which relates to interpretation involves the
translation of the adjective which qualifies 'fish' in the play-
within-the-play. Most translators agree on 'Men and lions,
partridges and eagles, spiders, geese, and antlered stags' but
disagree about the adjective qualifying fish and their habitat.
The Russian is 'molchalivye ryby, obitavshie v vode' (literally
'taciturn/reticent/ silent/unspeaking fish inhabiting/dwelling in
the water'). Variants include 'dumb fishes that used to dwell in
the water' (Koteliansky); 'silent fish living in the water'
(Alexander); 'the silent fishes of the deep' (Fen); 'silent fish that
inhabit the water' (Magarshack); 'the silent fishes dwelling in
the water' (Calderon); 'silent fish that dwell in the deep'

(Dunnigan); 'the silent fish inhabiting the deep' (Cook); 'wordless fish who swim beneath the wave' (Schmidt); 'silent fishes, denizens of the deep' (Hingley); 'the silent fish dwelling in the deep' (van Itallie); 'the silent fishes living in the sea' (Bristow); 'unfathomable fishes that dwell in the deep' (Stoppard) and the present translation's 'the unforthcoming fish that dwelt beneath the waters'.

Konstantin may be said to be guilty of the pathetic fallacy in attributing the silence of non-speech to fish when the silence can only be a human response to what it feels like to be deep underwater. The striking thing then is the silence, a fact on which most translators agree in referring to 'silent' fish. To that degree the image is slightly ridiculous but the only translations which set out to ironise and deflate the poetic pretensions of the play are those of Stoppard and Frayn. Stoppard's 'unfathomable' is a pun on measurement of depth (which applies to oceans) and inscrutability (which does not apply to fish). Frayn's is a pun on 'never appearing on the surface' (which might apply to certain deep-sea fish) and 'never revealing themselves in speech', based on the deliberately absurd notion of a talking fish (although there are examples of talking fish in Russian folk tales). Schmidt's 'wordless' fish may here also be intentionally absurd. The key issue consists in attitudes to the play-within-the-play. In the last examples, irony and bathos are established by the translation of a key word which seems designed to set the tone for the audience's reception of the play which follows. All other translations, with the exception of Koteliansky's, which just seems clumsy, leave matters more open.

The last example is from Act Four where, on two separate occasions, Nina refuses to be accompanied to the gate, stating that 'Loshadi moi stoiat u kalitki' ('My horses are standing/ waiting at the gate'). And then, after refusing food and insisting, again, that Konstantin does not accompany her, restates that 'Loshadi moi blizko . . .' ('My horses are close by . . .' [ellipses in original]). Nina behaves like someone who is exhausted from walking and unlike someone who has been hiring horse(s) and carriage at the inn for regular expeditions to the estate. In other words, there is the clear possibility that these horses (like the ones she imagines drawing her chariot in triumph in Act Two, p.32) are figments of her imagination. The questions to ask might be why she needs more than one horse in her undoubtedly straitened circumstances, or why does she insist (twice) on not being accompanied unless she knows that the horses do not exist? Konstantin's suicide is based partly on the belief that Nina has discovered reality whilst he still lives in a world of fantasy. But what if the reverse were true? To that extent, Nina's prolongation of her world of fantasy is crucially dependent on the existence, or non-existence, of the horses.

For most translators the horses which attend Nina at the gate are not only very real but have very material attachments such as carriages with four wheels and traps with two and even a cab. Moreover, the ellipses of indefinition are often omitted from the repetition. Only seven out of the following thirteen examples retain them: 'The horses are waiting for me at the gate. [. . .] My horses are not far off . . .' (Fen); 'The horses are waiting outside the gates. [. . .] The horses are close by . . .' (Koteliansky); 'My carriage is at the gate. [. . .] My carriage is quite near' (Hingley); 'My horses are waiting for me by the gate. [. . .] My horses are nearby' (Alexander); 'I've got a carriage waiting at the gate. [. . .] it's not far to where the carriage is . . .' (Schmidt); 'I've got a cab waiting at the gate. [. . .] My cab is close by' (Cook); 'My horses are waiting at the gate. [. . .] My horses are not far . . .' (Dunnigan); 'My trap is at the garden gate. [. . .] The trap is quite near . . .' (Calderon); 'My cab is waiting for me at the gate. [. . .] My cab is not far from here' (Magarshack); 'I have a carriage at the gate. [. . .] The horses are waiting . . .' (van Itallie); 'My horses are standing at the garden gate. [. . .] My horses are close by . . . (Bristow); 'My trap is waiting at the gate [. . .] Don't see me off. I'll go alone [repetition cut]' (Stoppard); 'My horses are at the gate [. . .] The horses are close by . . .' (Frayn).

It is important for a production to establish at this point whether Nina is one of Turgenev's 'homeless wanderers', like Bal'mont's seagull (both Turgenev and Bal'mont use the same adjective as Chekhov, 'bezpriutny', for shelterless/homeless), or is she rather a 'grande dame', who has the price of a carriage and pair about her for regular trips from town and is, therefore, not as 'homeless' as she claims to be? She has admittedly been barred from her father's house and seems to be patrolling the countryside but, at least, has a roof over her head at the inn where Konstantin has been standing under her window 'like a beggar' (p.62). The point would seem to be that neither of them is a beggar and neither is homeless but, like Masha and Sorin at other points in the play, indulge the notion of being so. Nina is, at least, out there in the storm and her appearance is described by Konstantin in decidedly expressionist terms: 'You've lost weight, and your eyes have got bigger' – an image reminiscent of Edvard Munch,[1] as well as of someone who has gone without food. But she is not starving and, when offered food, refuses it.

In a strange way, the person who is 'outside' at this moment, and whose skeletal frame is like that of the fit-up stage, is the person 'inside' in the warm. For this reason it is important that Masha's call at the opening of the act repeat his name four times – twice formally (Konstantin Gavrilovich) and twice familiarly (Kostya). In identifying Treplev by both a formal mode of address and the diminutive of his Christian name, Chekhov appears to be punning on the Russian for what the present translation renders as 'bare bones' and which in the original is '*skelet*' (skeleton). The Russian for a bare bone '*kost*' bears an uncanny resemblance to the diminutive for Konstantin – 'Kostya' – and would seem to establish a symbiotic link between Nina and Konstantin, during Act Four, as expressionistic shadows of the play's realistic appearances.

---

[1] *Edvard Munch*: a Norwegian painter and contemporary of Ibsen and Strindberg whose best-known work *Der Schrei* (The Scream) depicts in the foreground a ghost-like human presence in black on a wooden bridge, whose skull-like head, with starkly staring eyes and open mouth, is held between unnaturally elongated and prehensile hands. This figure is set against a background of two distantly defined figures in black and a brightly painted, swirling sunset over what might be a river or a lake and where the colours seem to echo and amplify the figure's agonised, fearful intensity. The whole is redolent of a nightmare and the mode of the painting is defined as 'expressionistic', Munch's name having become synonymous with that mode of representation.

Critical perspectives

Very little of critical length, or indeed substance, was written
about Chekhov's plays in English until about fifty years after
his death. One of the first in the field was David Magarshack
who, in his *Chekhov the Dramatist* (1952), paved the way for
others. He divided the plays into two categories: the earlier
plays which are described as those of 'direct action' and those,
from *The Seagull* onwards, of 'indirect action'. A notable
feature of the earlier plays in this analysis is that each has a
central character and an eponymous hero – *Platonov, Ivanov*.
The later plays, even a play with a name in its title, like *Uncle
Vanya*, is no longer a play directly concerned with a single fate
but, rather, with the fate of the group as a whole in which,
whilst some characters predominate, all are indirectly affected
by events.

In his discussion of *The Seagull*, Magarshack raised some of
the key issues which subsequent critics would return to. These
include the quality of the play in relation to those which
succeeded it; the status of the play-within-the-play and the
significance of the final scene. Magarshack's conclusion was
that 'the whole point of the play is Nina's struggle to overcome
her obsession [with the seagull as a premonition of her own
fate] and her triumph in the end. [. . .] On the realistic plane,
therefore, the "seagull" theme personifies Nina's tremendous
spiritual struggle against adversity and her final triumph over it'
(pp.190–2). He also suggests that what destroys Konstantin's
talent is his 'mother fixation' (p.194).

Magarshack's later book, *The Real Chekhov: An Introduction
to Chekhov's Last Plays* (1972), is less useful than his first in
being over-polemical and consisting to a large extent of plot
summaries couched rather oddly in the past tense when the
convention is to use the present. He interprets Konstantin's play
as Chekhov's attack on the Russian Symbolists and explains:

> He preferred to attack the Symbolist movement in an indirect
> way by making Konstantin [. . .] write a play based on the ideas
> of Vladimir Solovyov, poet, mystic and philosopher. [. . .] In his
> play Konstantin does his best to give a dramatic form to
> Solovyov's conception of the World Soul as, to quote Solovyov,

'a living being, the first of all living beings, *materia prima*, and the substratum of the created world'. Solovyov considered it 'the future potential mother of the world, existing outside God, corresponding as an ideal addition to the eternally actual Father of the three-in-one God'. As for the Fallen Angel (who also appears in Konstantin's play), Solovyov claimed that he had 'his sphere of action in the World Soul, a principle of a dual nature, placed as it is between God and the principle hostile to Him'. It was apparently Konstantin's intention to dramatise this cosmic conflict between the World Soul and the Fallen Angel. (p.22)

It was Magarshack who first made the point about the difficulty of translating Nina's confused reference to herself as both seagull and actress. Because of the lack of definite and indefinite articles in Russian, Magarshack stresses a grammatical point (which Richard Peace later queried) about the significance of the dash between 'I' and 'seagull' in Russian ('*Ia – chaika*') which, Magarshack suggests, must mean *the* seagull not *a* seagull (i.e. the one in Trigorin's projected fiction). He then rather spoils his point by ignoring the significance of the subsequent dash in '*Ia – aktrisa*' and translating it as *an* actress, rather than *the* actress, which logically it ought to be – a trap which the present translation does not fall into. It remains a moot point, however, as to whether Nina is thinking of Konstantin's dead seagull or Trigorin's literary seagull at this point, or whether she might not be harking back to her first identification of herself with the bird: 'But it's the lake that draws me here, like a seagull . . .'

The next significant contribution to the field of Chekhov studies in English was made by Maurice Valency in *The Breaking String: The Plays of Anton Chekhov* (1966) which contains valuable introductory material on the nineteenth-century historical, cultural and theatrical background to Chekhov's work. Weighing up the significance of the seagull symbol in the scales of the play's tragic events, Valency sets the human events of the play against the backdrop of nature:

The symbol of 'The Sea Gull' becomes clear. It is neither a question here of the girl, nor of the boy, but of the beauty of all living things – a wing against the sky, a girl's smile, a boy's pride – all the joy and beauty of life which are defaced at every moment by forces so blind and so careless that they cannot be called fate. In the wastefulness of nature there is no greatness, no tragedy, nor any trace of the heroic. What happens in the play is a very little thing. It is no more tragic than the plucking of a flower. (pp.54–5)

Valency also makes some pertinent comments on the play in terms of its debt to the Russian vaudeville tradition and its anticipation of what came to be known as the Theatre of the Absurd:

... what is specifically Chekhovian [. . .] is the author's awareness of the absurdity of the situation he has created, the irrationality of the characters' behaviour, the extravagance of the demands they make on one another, but most of all the hopeless inconsistency of their lives. Treplev's last words express concern that the sight of Nina as she leaves may upset his mother. Immediately after this charitable thought, he blows his brains out, without bothering his head about whether this will upset his mother or not. This is perhaps funny, an effect suitable for vaudeville. And perhaps this term serves better than another to characterise the sort of thing *The Sea Gull* was meant to be. It is a bitter vaudeville. (pp.156–7)

J.L. Styan's *Chekhov in Performance: A Commentary on the Major Plays* (1971) performed a valuable service in treating the plays, not simply as plays of ideas or subjects for critical interpretation, but as texts which have to be interpreted in performance on a line-by-line, scene-by-scene basis. Inevitably, the analysis involves assumptions about the play's dominant mood at critical points. Of Nina's reiteration of the lines from Konstantin's play in Act Four, Styan notes: 'Nina speaks the lines spontaneously, and with an assurance we did not hear on Treplev's stage in Act One [. . .] Before, her simpler, hesitant, mechanical rendering reduced the words almost to nonsense; now, the "cycle of sorrow" matches her experience [. . .] and, astonishingly, Treplev's supernatural portrait of a desolate world rings true' (p.86). Clearly this is not an impression that arises directly, in unmediated fashion, from the page but is a director's, or performer's, intepretative perspective.

One of the most positive assessments of Chekhov's work, which probably had more in common with Soviet views in tending to stress its overall optimism and faith in humankind, is that of Harvey Pitcher in *The Chekhov Play: A New Interpretation* (1973). However, in his discussion of *The Seagull*, Pitcher has a keen eye for the comic grotesque elements, just as Valency had noted a debt to Russian vaudeville. If there is a Gogolian influence in Chekhov's one-act 'jokes' such as *The Bear* and *The Proposal*, Pitcher also detects similar influences in *The Seagull*: 'Masha hands Medvedenko her snuff-box with the curt invitation "Help yourself", – just as the fat Ivan was wont to do in Gogol's comic *Tale of How Ivan Ivanovich Quarrelled with Ivan Nikiforovich*.' He also points to the 'deformalisation' of the play's structure through the use of 'pauses and inconsequential remarks, falling asleep, snoring, humming, superfluous phrases, anachronistic recollections, eating, playing games' (p.39).

The study also provides a useful discussion of the poetic/linguistic qualities of Konstantin's play and makes favourable comparison between quotations from it (in transliterated form) and 'the haunting couplet of Pushkin's *Ruslan and Liudmila* which Chekhov uses to very similar effect in [. . .] *Three Sisters*' (pp.62–3). At the same time, Pitcher's view of the enchanted lake is decidedly romantic. It is 'like a lake of folk legend, with magic powers for good and evil. It casts a spell over those who live round it [. . .] the more they turn back to the lake, with its poetry and its beauty, the harder it becomes to reconcile themselves to the prosaic realities of life and to shattered dreams' (p.48). He also believes that there

> is nothing neurotic about Nina [. . .] Nor was there anything wrong with her decision to give herself entirely to Trigorin, for she acted in the belief that she would be contributing to the sacred cause of Art. [. . .] Her idealism has disastrous consequences; but Nina survives, and breaks the spell of the lake and the seagull, because she is in the long run spiritually much healthier than the other three [i.e. Trigorin, Konstantin and Arkadina] [. . .] What is more important is that such talents as she has are not flawed by any personal defects. Talent is

appropriate to her, and this is the real beauty of the seagull (pp. 60–5).

One of the most important English researchers in the field of Chekhov studies during the past thirty years has been Donald Rayfield, whose first major study, *Chekhov: The Evolution of his Art*, appeared in 1975, followed by a revised and up-dated version in 1999, re-titled *Understanding Chekhov: A Critical Study of Chekhov's Prose and Drama*. This had been immediately preceded by his *Anton Chekhov: A Life* (1997) which, in having the advantage of access to archives formerly closed during the Soviet period, is destined to become the authoritative work on Chekhov the man for some time to come. Rayfield's view of *The Seagull* helpfully places it in the thematic context of Chekhov's short stories and, as an essentially experimental work, points to ways in which its characters and themes are developed in the later plays: 'It is the first "comedy" to take death in its stride: Nina's survival makes Treplev's death an accepted loss. The moral freedom of Ibsen and Hauptmann has found a new form that solves none of the questions, makes no divisions between good and evil, but leaves us with a feeling for the complexity and absurdity of life' (Rayfield: 1975, p.210).

In 1981, Jean-Pierre Barricelli edited a volume of critical essays which reprinted one by Robert Louis Jackson, who was among the first to take the theme and subject matter of Konstantin's play seriously. In an article entitled 'Chekhov's *Seagull*: The Empty Well, the Dry Lake and the Cold Cave', he traced the currency of symbols and images in the play as a whole, which amplified those introduced in the play-within-the-play in which the horror 'is, in a sense, an intuition; the self's forereading of its own tragic emptiness' (p.6). However, this reading is not extended to include Nina, whose love for Trigorin at the end is described as 'active love: love that is combined with a readiness to face life [. . .] it is love without illusions, love that seeks to envelop and not to be enveloped in warm self-oblivion. [. . .] The real knowledge of self, the blinding vision, the tragic perception [. . .] is granted to Nina. Her drama in its painful dialectic is symbolized in the complex image of the seagull; in its living and dead incarnations this

image enters her being as a "pro" and "contra"' (p.13). Those
horses which she says are waiting at the gate may, as was
suggested earlier, be fantasy horses but in Jackson's reading the
fantasy itself is real: 'Nina's horse – Pegasus, winged horse of
inspiration – stands ready to carry her away' (p.15).

One of the most interesting essays in the Barricelli anthology,
as it affects an interpretation of *The Seagull*, is Laurence
Senelick's 'Chekhov's Drama, Maeterlinck, and the Russian
Symbolists'. Senelick notes the non-naturalistic aspects of the
play which seem to him to have more in common with
Symbolism and Expressionism: 'Act I takes place in a wild part
of the park [. . .] It is a landscape of Böcklin or Munch, rather
than Levitan' (p.163). Of the significance of the offstage world
in Act Four, he states:

> . . . the shred of abandoned stage curtain flapping [. . .] with an
> unseen figure weeping behind it, the tapping watchman – all
> recall those intimations of mortality that encroach on
> Maeterlinck's sequestered figures. And as in Maeterlinck, the
> doors and windows take on special meaning, as apertures to
> another world. Treplev's uneasiness causes him to throw open a
> window that Arkadina insists be closed; later he opens the glass
> door, thus allowing the past, in the form of a muffled Nina, to
> enter, an encounter that impels him to suicide. (p.164)

He applies Henri Bergson's notion of time to the handling of
time in the play and concludes:

> For Chekhov, time is not so much duration as repetition, a
> scaled-down version of Nietzsche's 'eternal recurrence'. What is
> horrific is not that man must die and be thus rendered futile,
> but rather that he is condemned to lose himself in the routines
> of measured time. In this respect, Chekhov subscribes to
> Maeterlinck's well-known statement [. . .] asserting 'the
> impossibility of superior life within the confines of the humble
> and inevitable reality of daily life'. (p.165)

Senelick restates some of these ideas in his *Anton Chekhov*
(1985), echoing Harvey Pitcher's view of the enchanted lake
which 'can be felt as the spell of Sleeping Beauty's castle:
everyone who sets foot there is suspended in time, frozen in

place' (p.85) – a perception which seems very relevant to the play's final moments (see notes to pp.66–7). Like Valency, Senelick places the play in the context of its predecessors and describes Nina as 'a type of the victimised young girl, abandoned by her love and coming to a bad end [. . .] from Karamzin's *Poor Liza* (1792) onward. Often she is depicted as the ward of an older woman who, in her cruelty or wilful egotism, promotes the girl's downfall: many plays of Ostrovsky and Potekhin feature such a pair' (p.75). He also makes a subtle point about theatrical perspectives in Act One, where a theatre audience watches a play in which an audience watches a play on which a curtain descends before being raised again. The effect is to shift the gaze of the observer to the world of nature which now, from the viewpoint of eternity, observes the eccentric behaviour of the characters in the play (and, by implication, the theatre audience itself) through the eternal 'eyes' of the sun and the moon.

Richard Peace's *Chekhov: A Study of the Four Major Plays* (1983) makes some acute observations about the play's own naturalistic ironies and the way in which the genuine symbolist play is Chekhov's, rather than Konstantin's: 'Treplev's contempt for the trappings of the routine theatre and his insistence on presenting the play against a natural backdrop, seek in real theatrical terms to elevate the painted moon and lake into true originals, as if the second theatrical frame were a prism capable of transmuting image into reality [and although] Treplev's language may be elevated [. . .] his incantatory roll-call of nature's fauna finds a more sober counterpart in Chekhov's own symbolic use of the phenomena of the natural world . . .' (pp.18–19).

The above studies have in common the fact that they are full-length and have been produced by scholars who have access to the original Russian. There have, of course, been a number of other considerations of Chekhov's plays within the context of studies of European drama by scholars who have interesting things to say about Chekhov without having access to the original Russian. Among the most highly praised of recent studies has been Richard Gilman's *Chekhov's Plays – An Opening Into Eternity* (1995), in which he defines 'the reigning spirit of *The Seagull* [as] that of antiromanticism' (p.71). He also pursues interesting connections between Chekhov and Samuel Beckett and suggests that 'The restricted circumstances Beckett and Chekhov fashion for their plays [. . .] greatly resemble each other, for the artistic purpose of confinement is very much the same for both. [. . .] all of Beckett's characters and nearly all of Chekhov's are reduced to making their way, with what is left to them, through time' (p.80). Gilman also notes a technical innovation of Chekhov's which heightens the static effect of his plays and lessens their ostensible potential for dramatic change: 'From *The Seagull* on no play will fail to introduce well before the end of the first act everyone of any significance – [. . .] Nobody will come on stage later, bringing important news or actively furthering developments and so extending a line of more or less strictly unfolding narrative' (p.81). Gilman also makes the point that,

> Beginning with *The Seagull* things *said* in Chekhov's theater constitute most of the drama. Material occurrences have their own necessity and integrity, but in a shift with enormous consequences for the future of the stage, they mainly serve now to spring speech – the executive instrument of thought – into life, behaving as language's outcomes more than its causes. [. . .] That the play's chief physical eventfulness [. . .] takes place off stage, out of view, with most of the events not even made known until time has passed [. . .] deeply undercuts [. . .] melodramatic excess; it 'cools' the play down and so allows reflectiveness to control sensation; and it therefore enables us to experience the play more as a pattern of animate consciousness, a set of moral and psychic rhythms and discoveries, than as a narrow, emotionally overwrought tale. (p.96)

Finally, the student's attention is drawn to Eugene Bristow's edition of Chekhov's plays (1977), which includes a number of interesting critical essays as an appendix, including, with relevance to *The Seagull*, Nicholas Moravcevich's 'Chekhov and Naturalism: From Affinity to Divergence' and Thomas G. Winner's 'Chekhov's *Sea Gull* and Shakespeare's *Hamlet*: A Study of a Dramatic Device'.

The Seagull in production

Recent years have seen the publication of works which focus on the history of the production and critical reception of Chekhov's plays in the theatre, either focusing on specific, historically significant, productions (such as the Moscow Art Theatre production of *The Seagull* in 1898) or looking at the world history of Chekhov production in which those of *The Seagull* form a part. Of productions of Chekhov on the European and world stage, the definitive study is Laurence Senelick's *The Chekhov Theatre: A Century of the Plays in Performance* (1997). This, together with David Allen's *Performing Chekhov* (2000) leave very few stones unturned as far as significant productions of the plays world-wide are concerned.

The very first production of *The Seagull* was at the Alexsandrinsky (Alexandra) Theatre in St Petersburg in 1896. The details of this production have been exhaustively treated in the above-mentioned volumes and also by S.D. Balukhaty (1952) in his lengthy introduction to Stanislavsky's production score of the play, and by Peter Henry in an extended introduction to his edition of the Russian text of the play (1993) and by Donald Rayfield in his Chekhov biography (1997). The score itself has been analysed by David Richard Jones (1986) and by Balukhaty. The reception of these first productions is also described in the Translator's Introduction, pp.lxxx–lxxxiv.

Russian and Soviet productions

A general survey, together with an analysis of photographic stills, can be found in Gottlieb (1984). However, what has been missing to date has been public access to original reviews of the 1896 and 1898 productions. These have recently been published in Kuzicheva (1999). Among responses to the very first performance, that of one of Russia's leading theatre critics of the day, Aleksandr Kugel', is among the most interesting in that it highlights a sense of spiritual exhaustion in the play whilst expressing general irritation at the play's refusal to offer straightforward explanations of human behaviour:

> ... the characters wander about, neither quite in ecstasy, nor in half-sleep, and overall there is a feeling of some sort of decadent life-exhaustion [...] What is it that emerges from this ferment? The new forms which the *Seagull*'s heroes seek so avidly, or a slow, orderly 'degeneracy' of which [Max] Nordau speaks in his researches into new literary currents? I don't know. But to observe such plays is both painful and difficult, [...] Mr Chekhov's play is as dead as a wasteland [*pustynia*] [...] Why does the writer Trigorin live with an ageing actress? What is it that attracts him to her? Why does 'the seagull' fall in love with him? Why is the actress stingy? Why does her son write decadent plays? Why does the old man suffer from paralysis? Why is there a scene in which they drink and play lotto? Why does the doctor speak of a phial of ether exploding when a suicide has occurred? [On the actual night the actor referred, mistakenly, to a *bottle* of ether, the word having obscene connotations in Russian and producing uproarious laughter.] For what purpose does a young girl take snuff and drink vodka? [...] 'New forms' borrowed from the theory of Wagnerian 'leitmotives' amount to, more or less, the fact that each character has his or her own tiny peculiarity: the doctor is a Don Juan of 55 and everyone declares their love for him, the young lady takes snuff, the bailiff is constantly retailing anecdotes, the schoolteacher complains about expenses. [...] let's agree that it is a new form. But what's it in aid of? What does it clarify? Whose spiritual mood does it serve? What general idea does it put forward? [...] At the end of the evening a light comedy *A Happy Day* was staged. The performance was far from being first rate [...] with the exception of Ms Levkeyeva and Mr Varlamov ... (Kuzicheva, pp.104–5)

Another hostile review noted that, 'If the author of *Degeneration*, Max Nordau, had seen *The Seagull*, he would undoubtedly have declared it the best piece written for the boards this past quarter of a century! [...] *Degeneration* is the play's real title' (ibid., p.136).

As you will discover from reading the accounts of the first performance of *The Seagull*, the audience laughter which threatened to destroy the production originated during Vera Komissarzhevskaya's recital of Nina's speech in Konstantin's play. In subsequent performances, this led to the cutting of a repetition of lines from the play which Nina is requested to recite in Act Two. On the first-night, Nina answered Masha's request by reciting a few lines, with the inevitable consequences. The first-night laughter also led to the cutting of a bit of 'business' which the director, Karpov, had introduced in Act Four. Because Komissarzhevskaya was draped in a white garment during the Act One performance of Konstantin's play, at the point where she recites a section of it in Act Four, Karpov had her go across to the bed in Konstantin's study which has been made up for Sorin, take a sheet from it and swathe herself in it before delivering the monologue. The first-night audience's reaction was by this point uncontrollable. However, despite the first-night flop, resulting mainly from the constitution of an audience who were there for Levkeyeva's appearance in the afterpiece, *A Happy Day*, the reviews of the four remaining performances were much more positive and encouraging. When Komissarzhevskaya came to repeat her performance as Nina at her own theatre in St Petersburg, in 1905, the critic Yuri Beliaev said he actually preferred her first performance on account of its special quality of spiritual intensity.

A very sympathetic and appreciative review appeared in the *Samara Gazette*, when the play was staged in the provinces the following year. A.A. Smirnov, under the title 'Chekhov's Theatre of the Soul' compared *The Seagull* with Maeterlinck's *The Intruder* but also with Robert Browning's dramatic poems which a French critic had described as 'Théâtre d'âmes' (Theatre of the Soul). Chekhov's play was closest of all to the 'introspective dramas' of Robert Browning, according to Smirnov, with their absence of external action and the substitution of inner spiritual feeling. He also saw connections between Konstantin's play, Wilde's aestheticism and that of the Italian Gabriele d'Annunzio, 'who has attempted to create a book which does not imitate nature but manifests a continuation of it' (ibid., p.147).

In many respects, the European renown of *The Seagull* and Chekhov's own importance as a dramatist, derive from the play's revival by Nemirovich-Danchenko and Stanislavsky at the Moscow Art Theatre in December 1898, as part of their first season. It was a calculated risk which, fortunately, proved a triumph, but permission needed to be wrung from Chekhov to stage the play in the wake of its St Petersburg débâcle. Accounts of the production are available in the sources mentioned above, as is a translation of Stanislavsky's production score. A point worth noting is that, although the play was enormously popular with the public, it did not receive general critical acclaim. Many criticised the production's technical deficiencies as well as its general mood: 'The atmosphere of sickness, shattered nerves, hysterical fainting fits is electrified to such an extent that the spectator loses the criteria for evaluating the moral aspect of the characters and leads to the single question of life as somehow sick, cruel, despondent, absurd and unnecessary' (I.N. Ignatov in *Russikie vedomosti*, 1898, no.290, 20 December). When Chekhov saw the production, staged especially for him without décor in 1899, he was also critical of certain performances and singled out Stanislavsky as Trigorin and Roksanova as Nina for particular dispraise. The production was revived at the Moscow Art Theatre in 1905 but, altogether, was only given 63 performances prior to the revolution of 1917. Apart from productions by Tairov 1944, and Zavadsky in 1945, the play was not staged again in Russia until the 1960s.

Of the later productions, those staged by Anatoli Efros in 1966, Boris Livanov in 1968 and Oleg Efremov in 1970 and 1980, combined experimentation with orthodoxy whilst more recent, post-Soviet, productions have taken the play into the realms of postmodern 'performance art'. Because of the exigencies of a wartime Russian economy, Tairov staged his production of *The Seagull* with minimalist means as a 'concert performance' in black and grey velvet drapes, supplemented by a low platform, some armchairs and a grand piano on which was the effigy of a seagull in flight. Tairov's wife, Alisa Koonen, who was already forty-five, played the part of Nina.

The production was staged without make-up, costume or properties, utilising a mere third of the total script in order to bring out what Tairov saw as Chekhov's philosophy and the play's central theme: the struggle through new artistic forms to attain the highest truth, a kind of Platonic dialogue on art in which Nina's Act One soliloquy was accompanied by the music of Tchaikovsky played on the piano. Although critical opinion tended to be dismissive, the pianist Sviatoslav Richter approved of it. According to Laurence Senelick, whose account of *The Seagull* is referred to here, Zavadsky's 1945 production at the Mossoviet Theatre was intended as a reply to Tairov, but its Treplev was passive and static, more like Ibsen's Oswald, lacking any fervour and, by pausing after every word, 'this *Seagull* took four and a half hours to waddle to its conclusion' (Senelick: 1997, pp.195–9).

Anatoli Efros, who acquired something of a reputation as an *enfant terrible* during the more relaxed post-Stalin period of the 1960s, took exceptional liberties in his production of the play, breaking the action down into 'stations of the cross' (borrowed from German expressionist *stationendrama*) and replacing the scaffold stage with a real scaffold on which Konstantin was to be 'crucified'. In an attempt to bring the play up to date, Efros had his actors perform in such a way that, according to one critic, it was as if 'Chekhov had grown up in a communal apartment with one kitchen, one bathroom and forty residents, so noisy and hysterical a scene did they make. Conceiving Nina as a modern harpy, at one point Efros had her grab Trigorin's fishing rod and swish it furiously through the air in a way that 'hinted at a submerged sensuality [. . .] a predator awakening in this provincial miss' (ibid., pp.213–14).

Livanov's 1968 production at the Moscow Art Theatre tended to see the play as a film director might, mounted inside sparse, frequently changing décor into which short, film-like sequences were introduced. In the manner of Meyerhold, who had recently been rehabilitated and whose writings had just been published, Livanov played fast and loose with the text, repeating bits of dialogue, inserting extracts from other works by Chekhov and accompanying the performance throughout with the music of Scriabin. Of his conception of the play,

Livanov said: 'How many people realise that *The Seagull* is really a play about two seagulls, the white one, Nina, and the black one, Masha?' Immediately after Konstantin's suicide, Livanov had Masha burst into floods of silent weeping as the curtains closed on the unsuspecting lotto players (Gottlieb: 1984, pp.68–9). Livanov also explored parallels with *Hamlet*, and, like Okhlopkov's 1954 production of Shakespeare's play, staged *The Seagull* in décor suggestive of a prison, with Konstantin as Hamlet in white blouse and black cloak. Arkadina was played as a 'chill millionairess', Nina and Masha as emblems of heavenly and earthly love and with the latter as a betrayed Ophelia. During Trigorin's long speech to Nina at the end of Act Two, both dug for bait in flowerbeds centre stage (Senelick: 1997, p.218).

The bait-digging motif was resurrected by Efremov in his 1970 production at the Sovremennik Theatre in Moscow which was a polemical response to Livanov by someone who represented the spirit of non-orthodoxy in Soviet theatre of the 1960s. His 1980 production at the Moscow Art Theatre was designed by Valeri Levental as 'a symphony of light, a dance of curtains in flickering space [where] characters became part of the landscape [dissolving] in it and [dying] amidst the beauty of its indifferent world'. The director introduced the concept of 'transcendent nature' in which the main sound effect, the cry of a seagull, expressed 'the theme of an endless circling in search of something that might comfort the soul' (Gottlieb & Allain: 2000, p.35).

With the arrival of 'glasnost' and 'perestroika' in the late 1980s, followed by the collapse of the Soviet Union in the early 1990s, a degree of artistic freedom dramatically affected productions of plays, many of which were influenced by so-called 'postmodern' tendencies in Western Europe and America. As these affected productions of Chekhov's plays and *The Seagull* in particular, the trend towards 'deconstruction' was initiated by Yuri Pogrebnichko at his Theatre on Krasnaya Presnya, Moscow, in 1989, with a production entitled *Why Did Konstantin Shoot Himself?* which he followed up, in 1993, with *There's a Theatre for You . . . and Beyond That Empty Space (based on A.P. Chekhov's comedy 'The Seagull')*. In this second version, Pogrebnichko envisioned:

a magical, absurd space, full of bizarre and evocative
juxtapositions and a weirdly wonderful humour comprising
visual and linguistic punning, deliberate misemphasis and
misunderstanding, silliness, naughtiness, and surreally realized
metaphor. Thus the spirits of Shakespeare, Napoleon and Caesar
materialize from the text of Treplev's play and linger throughout
to eavesdrop and generally get in the way. For instance, in Act
Four Treplev assures Nina not to be afraid, that no one will
come in, upon which immediately enters Caesar, who sits down
to observe Treplev's and Nina's final drama ... (Richard
Borden, 'Chekhov on the Russian Stage' in D. Clayton (ed.),
Chekhov Then and Now, p.98)

With a further echo of *Hamlet* and the famous 'Mousetrap'
scene, a central symbol of this production was an actual
mousetrap which one of the stagehands swung on a string at
the play's commencement, like the pendulum of a clock, whilst
imitating the tick-tock sounds by clicking his tongue. This motif
then spawned a whole array of felt-covered mice which, at
punningly suitable moments of dialogue, were drawn like
conjuror's props out of waistcoat and trouser pockets. When
Konstantin demanded 'new forms' of art, plush new mice
appeared, as did ones apparently smelling of heliotrope during
Trigorin's soliloquy at the point where he refers to that
particular scent. The production concluded with Trigorin
breaking into an idiotic grin at the news that Konstantin has
shot himself and tweaking Dorn's nose (ibid., pp.98–9).

Taking his cue from Pogrebnichko, Sergei Solovyov, at the
Moscow Taganka Theatre in 1994, turned the stage into a
malarial swamp of real water and introduced rowing boats and
bicycles, a speeded-up film performance of Nina's awful acting
on the provincial stage, a crippled Sorin who is carried about
by Shamrayev only to be dropped at moments such as the
latter's rendition of 'Bravo, Silva!', in Act Two, when he
needed his hands free to gesticulate. The production also
boasted naked men, a shirtless Trigorin fishing up old boots
and a bouquet of flowers during his long soliloquy to Nina,
and the final suicide of Konstantin staged in a rowing boat in
the middle of the on-stage lake.

Also in 1994, V. Akhadov at the New Experimental Theatre

in Magnitogorsk staged what was considered one of the most interesting Chekhov productions of the decade in which he conceived *The Seagull* as a rural vaudeville staged in the style of late-nineteenth-century popular entertainment, with unexpected transformation scenes, circus tricks, and with the action unfolding as a continuous fairground side-show. Each of the characters was emblematically masked, Arkadina as an over-ripe teenager (the part she claims she can play at the beginning of Act Two), Trigorin as a comic country bumpkin, Sorin as 'the kind father', and Nina as a snub-nosed, innocent and well-meaning simpleton. The play also introduced a French personal secretary for Arkadina, one Colette, whose non-comprehension of Russian came to suggest the incomprehensibility of everyone's behaviour as seen through her eyes. Colette viewed everything around her as if she were a spectator at a play, even applauding the 'performance' which Arkadina and Trigorin give in Act Three as if at a rehearsal. She received report of Treplev's suicide in the same fashion, applauding as if it were all part of a game, a carefully staged 'act'. Konstantin's own play was staged in the background, with the audience taking over the foreground, getting on with their own affairs seemingly oblivious of Nina. However, during the course of the subsequent action, it was as if the play had become 'the latest thing' and characters would hum, or recite snatches of its dialogue and in the final act, everyone waved a set of wings and declaimed the monologue about the world soul. Arkadina, by this time, had donned a hat with huge seagull feathers and, after the Act Four supper, the group gathered to watch a reprise of Konstantin's play but, this time, with Arkadina in the leading role.

In 1995, at the Volgograd Theatre for Children and Young People, V. Granatov staged a production of *The Seagull* in the style of a 'black comedy' in which many of the scenes were realised as dreams and with the accent on Konstantin's spiritual illness. The characters were dressed as French aristocrats of the eighteenth century and the mise-en-scène was in the style of elegant figurines. All the men were performed as shameless flatterers and all the women as empty-headed creatures who passed from the embrace of one man to the next. During the final act, the characters threw off their lavish costumes and reappeared bedraggled and aged. Dorn returned from abroad having gone blind, to suggest that the character had been metaphorically blind hitherto, whilst the freedom which Nina achieved transformed her, instantly, into Arkadina's double. Again, in the manner of Meyerhold, who had a penchant for introducing mute and mysterious characters into his productions, the principal character in this production was 'A Person in Black' who appeared as Yakov at the outset and became the self-styled director of everything on stage as a 'decadent symphony'. It was as if the Devil in Konstantin's play had taken on a life of his own, intervening in the action, turning the characters into marionettes subject to his will and, finally, shooting Treplev who died with a smile on his lips as if glad to be free of these cursed 'spirits'.

Another attempt to stage the play as a rural vaudeville was made in 1998 by A. Khermanis at the New Drama Theatre in Riga, Latvia. Normal forms and proportions were subjected to radical revision with Sorin's estate reduced to the size of a toy farm and with marionette doubles for each of the characters who also related to each other in an openly parodistic manner. Each character was made up to look like a Russian writer but in a grotesquely stylised manner. Konstantin looked like Pushkin, Masha like Marina Tsvetaeva, Medvedenko like Esenin, and with Trigorin as a hybrid consisting of Dostoevsky's beard, Gorky's hat and Tolstoy's peasant shirt. However, unlike the Abakhov production which sustained the parodistic element to the end, even including Konstantin's suicide, the characters in this production progressively discarded their comic exteriors to reveal the suffering human beings beneath. At the end, instead of shooting himself, Treplev took off like a bird 'as if on some symbolic flight of the soul' (E.A. Andrushchenko (ed.), *Kritika, Dramaturgia, Teatr* (Kharkov: 'Viktoriia', 1999), pp.110–20).

For the Third International Theatre Olympics, held in Moscow in 2001, Andrei Zholdak staged a production called *Experiment: Seagull* in the building where the Art Theatre's 1898 production was staged. The *Plays International* Moscow correspondent, John Freedman, described it as 'a show about the near impossibility of being an artist or, at least, a sensitive person, in an age when we are bombarded by refuse, by superfluous detail, by noise and technology. This is reflected in Kolio Karamfilov's effective set mixing junk and random domestic details around a make-believe lake. Rocks and trash tumble down twisted drainpipes; automatons work on a conveyor belt behind an occasionally transparent screen; and characters "swim" in the lake on oversized skateboards as splashing sounds echo through the hall. Zholdak attacked *The Seagull* with insolence and reverence combined, and emerged with an often fascinating show' (July and August 2001, p.33).

The world-renowned Maly Drama Theatre of St Petersburg, under its artistic director Lev Dodin, staged a production of *The Seagull* in 2001 in the wake of productions of *The Cherry Orchard* and *Platonov* which had previously toured abroad. Although they do not feature in Chekhov's play, bicycles featured prominently in this particular production, whether ridden up and down planks on either side of the stage or over a grassy area suspended above a pool of water. The scene in which Arkadina replaced Konstantin's bandage was staged seated on a heap of bicycles, whilst the lotto game was played by the participants seated astride bikes which they pedalled on the spot (*Plays International*, September 2001).

Lastly, mention should be made of a ballet, based on *The Seagull* and staged at the Bolshoi Theatre in 1980 to music by Rodion Shchedrin, with décor by Valeri Levental and directed by Maia Plisetskaia who also danced the role of Nina. The conductor was Aleksandr Lazarev. The ballet consisted of twenty-four preludes plus three interludes and a postlude. The content and style were influenced by the original reception of the play in 1896 and the resulting press criticism. These were specifically evoked in three interludes which punctuated the development of the plot and were performed by the corps-de-ballet in the form of crowd scenes. They depicted a 'faceless, monochrome, soulless audience – the men in evening dress and white gloves, the women in identical striped dresses all holding fans' and leering, sniggering and gloating to the musical accompaniment of triangles and other instruments which reproduced appropriately mimetic sounds (Emma Polotskaia,

'*The Seagull* at the Bolshoi', in D. Clayton (ed.), op. cit., p.253). In the absence of dialogue, a croquet game was introduced at the beginning of Act Two which became a form of pas de deux between Trigorin and Nina illustrating their flirtation. The seagull motif took on some of the elements of a ballet such as *Swan Lake*, in the sense that Plisetskaia danced the roles of both a seagull and Nina. The resolution of the two images was achieved in the final act when, on entering Treplev's study, 'her figure projects two shadows resembling wings. Then, with the noise of the rain, thunder and lightning growing in the background, her shadow merges for a moment with that of Treplev, and this combined shadow again resembles the outline of a bird. It is as if two fates have combined only to break apart and go in different directions. Once more, to conclude the symbolism, this time only with reference to Treplev, the seagull image reappears when he shoots himself and falls face down, his arms outstretched like wings' (ibid., p.254).

Productions in Britain

The best sources for information on British productions of Chekhov are Emeljanow (1981), who also includes some American productions, Allen (2000) and Miles (1993). The first-ever production of a Chekhov play in Britain was of *The Seagull* at the Royalty Theatre, Glasgow, on 2 November 1909, which produced a thoughtful critical response from reviewers: 'Certainly it is a play full of interesting commentaries on life and art – a drama of realism which ought to be seen by everyone who is a serious student of the stage,' ran an unsigned review in the Glasgow *Evening Times*. A similarly unsigned notice in the *Glasgow Herald* referred to the play's 'odd and elusive symbolism full of characters who are possessed by the passionate desire of living intensely, and at the same time are foiled by circumstances and their own natures and compelled to stagnate instead. [. . .] The futility of life and effort is strongly borne in on one, but the whole is illumined by comedy, and the humanity of the play is so warm and appealing that it somehow touches and interests more than it depresses . . .' (Emeljanow pp.86–8). The first production in England was at

the Fortune Theatre, London, in 1919. In his review, the
leading theatre critic of the day, James Agate, described it as
'one huge haystack of despondency, with not more than three
tiny needles of glinting humour' (James Agate, *Red Letter
Nights* (London: Jonathan Cape, 1944), pp.97–8).

A revival at the Little Theatre in London, directed by Philip
Ridgeway, starred John Gielgud as Konstantin and Valerie
Taylor as Nina. J.C. Squire, in criticising the play and the
production, may have hit on a central truth when he wrote:
'But does a soul in the audience mind in the least when
Konstantin, the young man, the central figure in the play,
shoots himself at the climax of his tragedy? Nobody turns a
hair. Nothing has died because nothing has lived . . .'
(Emeljanow, op. cit., p.282). Another critic compared the same
production to Shakespeare's *A Midsummer Night's Dream* in
which 'the bemused lovers chase one another over the scene
. . .' and 'The effect of all this is a mingling [. . .] of the
ludicrous with the pathetic. Whatever his defects, Chekhov is
supreme in this medley. He leads to nothing, concludes about
nothing, has no message' (ibid., p.284).

The next significant British production of *The Seagull* was by
the eminent Russian émigré director, Theodore Komisarjevsky
(brother of the first interpreter of the role of Nina) at the New
Theatre, London, in May 1936. Much was expected of this
production, with its all-star cast, especially following the
ground-breaking productions of Chekhov plays which
Komisarjevsky had staged at the Barnes Theatre during the
1920s. This new production used many of the actors with
whom 'Komis' had previously worked, including Gielgud as
Trigorin, Edith Evans as Arkadina and Peggy Ashcroft as Nina.
The production was generally very well-received, especially for
its sense of ensemble, but an otherwise enthusiastic James Agate
was critical of Gielgud whose Trigorin 'was a shade too young
and not raffish enough. Trigorin is worse than a second-rate
novelist, he is a third-rate character. [. . .] The actor wanted
here was [one] who would have made a mouthful of Nina, just
as the wolf did of Red Riding Hood . . .' (James Agate, *More
First Nights* (London: Victor Gollancz, 1937), p.275).
Commenting on what they saw as the funereal pace of the

production, the *New English Weekly* announced, ironically, that 'the production [. . .] is beyond description soulful; and an invisible hassock for the reverential is supplied to every seat . . .' (Senelick: 1997, p.161).

A production at the Lyric Theatre, Hammersmith, in 1949, starred Paul Scofield and Mai Zetterling in which 'Scofield finely suggested [a] sense of possible genius in the throes of self-release' but where Zetterling as Nina 'was slightly hampered by her Swedish accent' (Audrey Williamson, *Theatre of Two Decades* (London: Rockliff, 1951), pp.206–7). A further revival at the Queen's Theatre, London, in March 1964 was directed by Tony Richardson with Peggy Ashcroft, now as Arkadina, and with Nina played by Vanessa Redgrave. The cast also included Peter Finch as Trigorin, Peter McEnery as Konstantin and George Devine as Dorn. According to Gordon McVay, 'Many found [Redgrave] magnificent, particularly in the last act. Redgrave's conception of Nina in Act Four differed fundamentally from Ashcroft's in 1936. Whereas Ashcroft considered Nina "destroyed", Redgrave declared: "The audience must believe that Nina has found a source of strength which will pull her through, but it will take some time before she really *is* strong" ' (in Miles: 1993, pp.93–4). The staging of the offstage meal in Act Four was a memorable feature of this production as the cast tucked into real food at a properly laid table in the wings. The effect of the contrast during Konstantin's and Nina's final confrontation between those who are spiritually hungry, as opposed to those who are physically so, was strongly communicated.

Jonathan Miller had two attempts at staging *The Seagull* – at the Nottingham Playhouse in 1968 and at the Chichester Festival Theatre in 1973 – with the same designer, Patrick Robertson, but on the second occasion with Irene Worth as Arkadina and Robert Stephens as Trigorin. A memorable moment in the production was Konstantin's pre-suicide preparation, as performed by Peter Eyre, which took up a whole seven minutes of stage time. As Miller, like Chekhov a doctor by profession, explained:

> I approach Chekhov on the stage with a certain amount of clinical detail. By clinical I do not mean pathological, I am

interested in the nuances of physical behaviour [. . .] People who
are preparing for suicide often leave traces, in order to let others
know how injured they have been. [. . .] In my production,
Treplev begins by tearing up the papers and putting some in the
wastepaper basket; then he stuffs some in his pocket, so that
when the body is found, traces of his own romantic failure as a
writer will be found on him. Then, he looks around the room,
to see that everything is set as he wants it. He suddenly
remembers he had given some water to Nina; the glass is still
half-full. He drinks down the rest, shakes out the drops and
places the glass on top of the carafe, so that no trace of her
presence will be left. Then he checks the room once more.
When he is ready, he goes out to shoot himself. (Allen: 2000,
pp.180–1)

April 1981 saw a unique production of *The Seagull* staged at
the Royal Court Theatre, London, in a 'new version' by the
Irish playwright Thomas Kilroy. The characters were renamed,
with Arkadina becoming Isobel Desmond, Nina becoming Lily,
Trigorin Mr Aston, Dorn Dr Hickey, and with the entire action
moved to the Desmond Estate in the West of Ireland. The
astonishing thing was that the transfer appeared to work
amazingly well with first-rate performances from Anna Massey
(Isobel), Alan Rickman (Aston) and Harriet Walter (Lily), in a
play where social tensions on an Anglo-Irish estate between the
anglicised residents and native Irish, in particular Tony Rohr's
estate manager James (Shamrayev), gained political sharpness in
Max Stafford-Clark's intelligent and well-paced production.
Konstantin's play was recast in the form of an Irish
mythological work redolent of Yeats' 'Celtic Twilight' phase
with Lily as Macha, Queen of Uladh (instead of the World
Soul), 'dressed in a long green robe and wearing a kind of
crown in the style of contemporary nationalist representations
of Ireland'. Kilroy himself provides an interesting account of his
work on the play in Gottlieb & Allain: 2000, pp.80–90.

At Glasgow's Citizens Theatre, in 1984, director Philip
Prowse recognised that *The Seagull* seemed to have a lot in
common with the world of Jean Renoir's classic 1930s film, *La
Règle du Jeu* and 'needed long, alfresco dinner parties and a lot
of moody silence if it was to achieve that feeling of a closed

world in which suicide is in the end only an example of very
bad weekend manners' (Sheridan Morley in *Plays and Players*).
Taking up the film likenesses, Giles Gordon, in the *Spectator*,
thought the opening was reminiscent of Alain Resnais's classic
1950s film, *L'Année Dernière à Marienbad*, or a game where
no one has told the players what the rules are. According to
Rosemary Say in the *Daily Telegraph* (29.04.84), 'Maria
Aitken [made] Arkadina a restless, flame-haired beauty smartly
interrupting Nina's first impulsive rush towards Trigorin and
kicking the dead seagull off the trestle stage with callous
disdain.' Konstantin's suicide occurred on stage in full view of
the audience and Prowse, who also designed the production,
created a funereal study for Act Four with the stuffed seagull
displayed prominently and with the white, bentwood chairs of
earlier acts replaced by black ones.

Charles Sturridge's production at the Lyric Theatre,
Hammersmith, in 1985 excited a good deal of critical
attention for the way in which it emphasised a degree of
comedy, even farce in the play. His Nina was another member
of the Redgrave dynasty, Natasha Richardson, and his Trigorin
was John Hurt. Whilst managing to bring out comic aspects of
the play, critics felt that the production also struck one or two
false notes. Irving Wardle expressed doubts about the moment
in Act Three 'when Arkadina [Samantha Eggar] falls on her
knees and embraces Trigorin, passionately declaring her
physical attachment to him, [and] fumbles with his trousers. Is
she really planning to seduce him in the dining-room?' (*The
Times*, 27.04.85). Critics were also doubtful about the ending,
where Sturridge had Masha overhear Dorn's announcement of
Konstantin's death, get up hurriedly from the lotto table, and
vomit. This idea was dropped when the production transferred
to the Queen's Theatre with some cast changes – Jonathan
Pryce as Trigorin and Vanessa Redgrave (Natasha Richardson's
real-life mother) as Arkadina. According to Sheridan Morley,
Redgrave played Arkadina 'as a languid cigarette-smoking
Bloomsbury figure closer to Virginia Woolf than to the
barnstorming Russian touring actress one might have
anticipated' (*Punch*, 21.08.85). It was also a production in

which 'Nina's last speech [. . .] acquire[d] the chilling force of a
Beckett monologue', according to Victoria Radin in the *New
Statesman* (09.08.85).

The 1990s saw a succession of revivals of *The Seagull*,
including some striking provincial ones. A production by Terry
Hands at the Swan Theatre, Stratford-upon-Avon, in November
1990, with Simon Russell Beale as Konstantin and Susan
Fleetwood as Arkadina, used the present translation by Michael
Frayn. In his review, the *Guardian* critic, Michael Billington,
noted the appropriateness of a remark Thornton Wilder once
made about Chekhov's plays to the effect that 'Nobody hears
what anybody else says. Everybody walks in a self-centred
dream.' Billington went on to describe 'Amanda Root's sterling
Nina. Initially she is the epitome of provincial go-getting as she
jumps with cat-like energy around the fit-up stage and
instinctively primps her hair at Trigorin's approach; by the last
act she has become a pale, ravaged figure acknowledging both
her own second-rateness and the illusory nature of fame.' Susan
Fleetwood's Arkadina was 'a monumental egotist who treats
life as a walking melodrama'. Konstantin, as played by Russell
Beale, was 'at first a petulant, nervy figure desperate for
affection and wracked by Oedipal hatred of Trigorin. By the
last act this Konstantin has changed into an obsessive solitary
[who] tears up his stories and gazes silently at his desk in wan
contemplation of the writer he might have been. [. . .] The real
tragedy of this play [. . .] is that the hardened egoists survive
while those who remain open to experience are patently
doomed' (Michael Billington, *One Night Stands* (London: Nick
Hern Books, 1993), pp.341–2). Rosalind Miles thought that
'never before ha[d] a production so persuasively conveyed its
peculiar combination of hysteria and boredom, forcing the
audience to share the characters' sensation of being trapped in
a bad dream. [. . .] As Arkadina, Susan Fleetwood [was] a
miraculous study of the obsessional narcissism fuelling every
monster mother. [. . .] Simon Russell Beale's doomed Konstantin
clearly sees that she neither knows nor cares if he lives or dies,
and in the existential void he cannot survive. [. . .] Masha [Katy
Behean] here played with such ferocious conviction [. . .] is ably
supported by Graham Turner [as] a brave Medvedenko trailing

the contemporary equivalent of the C&A anorak and the whiff of HP sauce: it takes balls to play a man being publicly castrated on stage every night . . .' (*Plays and Players*, March 1991).

Anthony Clark's production at the Birmingham Repertory Theatre, in 1990, picked up on those expressionist elements in the play detected by some critics. Liz Fjelles's setting, with its long reflection of a low sun on the lake, and on the floor and curtains of the interior scenes, put critics in mind of the paintings of Edvard Munch, a 'landscape of raucous colours within swirling topographical lines'. This expressionism was also felt in some of the performances: 'Michelle Wade's Masha opens the play in a hysterical outburst that bellies out during the course of the evening to an alcoholic dementia which is at once funny and savage. In this actress's ability to let her mood fragment her features lies an echo of Munch's famous *Scream* . . .' (Claire Armitstead, *Financial Times*, 22.02.90). Konstantin's play was performed to the cacophonous accompaniment of household implements and the on-stage audience's loud slapping of imaginary swarms of lakeside midges. Critics were especially struck by the conception of Masha in this production played as a 'roguish Ophelia snorting snuff as though she had shares in the company' (Jeremy Kingston, *The Times*, 22.02.90) and turning her misery 'into a bitterly comic routine, and [managing] to make snuff taking look as deliberately hostile an act as hurling a brick through a drawing-room window' (Paul Taylor, *Independent*, 23.02.90).

At the National Theatre, in July 1994, John Caird staged a revival in a translation by Pam Gems and with music by Dominic Muldowney, in which Judi Dench acted a memorable Arkadina as someone simultaneously hilarious, terrifying and heartbreaking, according to Irving Wardle. Paul Taylor captured some of the hilarity: 'Looking like a bad-tempered pug in a turban, Judi Dench gives a toweringly comic performance as Arkadina [. . .] [tackling Trigorin] to the floor and grappl[ing] with him there in an undignified sexual scrimmage emitting little orgasmic cries. [. . .] Dench turns the scene where she re-bandages her son's head after his suicide attempt into a hilarious slapstick routine. Starting grudgingly, she gradually warms to the job and then becomes ludicrously absorbed in getting it just right, racing round the boy's head with lengths of bandage as though he were a maypole, or having to unravel it all so that she can reach a pair of scissors she'd recently been cutting grapes with' (*Independent*, 09.07.94).

A production with an English cast by the Georgian director, Robert Sturua, which toured the provinces in 1995 was greeted by critics with such opprobrium that it never reached the London stage as planned. However, this production of *The Seagull* received less than its due. Although rather weakly cast, with the exception of Arkadina and Konstantin, it was a very volatile, tactile and simply-staged production. The dominant motif appeared to be gravitational force, both emotional and scientific, with spurts of emotion and flights of aspiration viewed from an ironically rationalist angle. The theme might be stated as 'what goes up, must come down' and was amusingly introduced at the outset by having a paper dart thrown on from the wings which, like Nina's and Konstantin's trajectories throughout the play, fluttered through the air before nose-diving to the ground. The spirit of Isaac Newton reigned over Act Two in particular as, from time to time, and interspersed with the conversation, apples would occasionally drop to the stage floor from an invisible tree, to be casually collected by members of the cast and placed in a wooden box downstage centre.

In a production at the Donmar Theatre, in 1997, directed by Stephen Unwin in a translation by Stephen Mulrine, Cheryl Campbell's Arkadina 'thundered round the room after Trigorin in Act Two, mounted him on the sofa and shook him until his head rocked like a puppet' (*Times Literary Supplement*, 29.08.97, p.20). Peter Hall's 1997 Old Vic production in a version by Tom Stoppard, with Felicity Kendal and Michael Pennington as Arkadina and Trigorin, seemed remarkably staid in comparison. Stoppard's version was used by Jude Kelly in her production at the West Yorkshire Playhouse in 1998. Perhaps because Ian McKellan was cast as Dorn, critical attention was drawn to what seemed to be the special prominence of this character in the play as a whole, although Clare Higgins made a fine Arkadina in a production which John Peter in the *Sunday Times* described as one of the greatest

Chekhovs he had seen. The same critic was less impressed with Adrian Noble's production at the Swan Theatre, Stratford-upon-Avon, in 2000, with Penelope Wilton as Arkadina, Richard Johnson as Dorn, Richard Pasco as Sorin and Nigel Terry as Trigorin. He felt that Terry's Trigorin was mistakenly played as 'a big, lean, grizzled hunter, fifty if he is a day, made gaunt and slightly crabby by middle age'. However, whilst normally disliking the introduction of music into Chekhov's plays, 'here, when Dorn withdraws to a corner and listens, with the unaffected pleasure of the old, to his crackling old opera records, you experience a true Chekhovian moment. Art can be a consolation, which is a moral value' (*Sunday Times*, 06.02.00).

Other productions

In his summarising retrospective of twentieth-century productions of *The Seagull*, apart from those already mentioned here, Laurence Senelick picks out Pitoëff's two Parisian productions in 1922 and 1939, describing them as 'threnodies, with Treplev a type of martyred artist and Nina an ethereal muse' (in Gottlieb & Allain, p.180). Otomar Krejca's production at the Narodni Divadlo, Prague, in 1960, was memorable amongst other things for its designs by Josef Svoboda, with projected images on a cyclorama achieving what amounted to Konstantin's 'dream' of new stage forms through a bare stage and pools of light and leaf patterns.

A production of *The Seagull* in Berlin, in 1969, by the Romanian director Lucian Pintilie, seemed a deliberate attempt to break with socialist realist norms imposed in his home country at that time. With an apparent debt to the Soviet director Meyerhold, who had been suppressed in Stalin's Soviet Union, a practically empty stage deployed a sand-coloured platform and focused on the physical passions of the protagonists. When Pintilie was forced to emigrate, he re-staged the production in Minneapolis during the 1980s. The ideas in it, according to Robert Brustein, came at the audience 'like a shower of meteors'. The play began with the final act and then continued in flashback as perceived through the mind of a hallucinating Konstantin. Described as 'a bizarre and irritating, yet always absorbing and provocative experiment' in the tradition of his Romanian countryman Andrei Serban, and Peter Brook, Pintilie's production was:

> Chekhov without walls – a glittering dreamscape of memory and desire. Radu Boruzescu's setting is a gorgeous environment – a burnished metallic mirror that becomes transparent to reveal a ghostly Nina surrounded by a forest of birches (and later Treplev's improvised stage covered with twigs and branches) – and Miruna Boruzescu's gauzy lace, linen, crinoline, and velvet costumes, festooned with boas and ostrich-feathered hats, are equally shimmering. Whatever is implicit in the play, Pintilie makes explicit. When [Arkadina] admits she has never read a word of her son's work, Treplev is behind her to absorb the insult. [. . .] Treplev's first suicide attempt is performed before the audience. And when Treplev catalogues his mother's faults ('She's a psychological case'), he speaks the indictment within earshot as [Arkadina] floats lazily on a swing. 'How lovely it used to be – do you remember?' asks the distraught Nina, and the stage transforms in preparation for the beginning of the play – for the ending, too, because the fourth act is repeated in its entirety, creating a rather tedious sense of *déjà vu*. At the climax, Nina is surrounded by [Arkadina] and Masha, who stain her face with black makeup, dress her in a feathered seagull costume, and crucify her on Treplev's stage – a stage that trolleys behind the panels immersed in fog and smoke, with Nina screaming, to the accompaniment of high-pitched electronics, 'Now I am a real actress.' Having witnessed this, there's nothing left for Treplev to do but burn his manuscript and end his life. (Robert Brustein, *Who Needs Theatre*, London: Faber and Faber, 1989, pp.90–1)

For Andrei Serban's own production, staged in Japan in 1980, the set consisted of a lake of real water, with real rocks, birch trees, grass and flowers on which was a platform stage shaped like a seagull. During Act One, the workmen went for a swim in full view of the audience, and the moon of Konstantin's play was reflected on the water's surface, which, by Act Four, had developed real waves into which Konstantin cast the torn sheets

of his manuscript, turning the surface white. After shooting
himself, he fell face down in the water among the scattered
pages (Allen: 2000, p.135).

Antoine Vitez's 1984 Paris production was one of the first
attempts to impose a 'postmodern' perspective on the work.
Konstantin's stage was a low platform, like a landing stage on
a lake, placed centre-stage and level with the proscenium arch
and with the lake located in the audience. The on-stage
audience then watched Nina's performance from the front,
whilst the theatre audience saw it from the back and, when the
on-stage curtain was lowered, could see Nina changing her
costume 'backstage'. This 'mirror effect' turned the audience in
the theatre into a 'double voyeur' (Senelick: 1997, pp.280–1).
The Italian, Roberto Ciulli, in 1984, 'reduced the play to a
series of startling, evocative images; a blind Sorin feeling his
way through velvet curtains, Nina dressed as Pierrot tied to a
stake, the lotto game played against a mountain of suitcases
around an empty bedstead' (Gottlieb & Allain, p.182).
Hirowatari Tsunetoshi's 1993 production staged Konstantin's
play as a dance drama 'with five nude young men moving
exotically around Nina to symbolize cosmic forces of evil
demons or fate' (Senelick: 1997, p.331).

Luc Bondy's production, staged at the Vienna Burgtheater
with Gert Voss as Trigorin and Jutta Lampe as Arkadina and
seen at the Edinburgh Festival in 2001, received mixed reviews.
Set in 'an indeterminate modern world of sun-glasses, high
heels and refrigerators' (*Guardian*, 31.08.01), the spirit which
hovered over the production seemed to be that of Stanislavsky,
the cast's 'unhurried acting being rooted in naturalism'
(*Independent on Sunday*, 02.09.01). The production was set
'before a drab blue wall upon which a crude painting of Sorin's
lake remains projected even when outdoors turns to indoors, or
a fragmentary dining room becomes the ugly attic, complete
with bits of paper pegged to a washing line, that serves as the
aspiring author Kostia's study. But this weird set helps to
desentimentalise a play still sometimes staged as prettily
atmospheric and Chekhovian' (*The Times*, 31.08.01). However,
according to the critic in the *Daily Telegraph*, 'Bondy [. . .] sets
the action on a hideous set that looks more like a grim

industrial warehouse than a country house, with a ghastly semi-abstract painting of the beautiful lake daubed on the walls. [...] The costumes [...] are a bizarre parade of twentieth-century fashion, ranging from turn-of-the-century formality, through Twenties cocktail dresses and the Fifties bohemian look, to modern suits. The actress, Arkadina, wears shades, her lover, Trigorin, has a pipe permanently clamped between his teeth, and the characters help themselves to drinks from a fridge. [...] The effect is to create an ugly, distracting mess. Where and when are these people meant to be living? In an arrogant, directorial Nowheresville, that's where' (31.08.01). Nevertheless most critics agreed on some fine acting from the two principals and from Maria Hengge as Masha.

The first American production of *The Seagull* was staged in New York in May 1916. Some critics were impatient, such as the reviewer in *Nation* for whom it was hard 'to take seriously the neurasthenic maunderings which in this play are paraded in the guise of dramatic complications. [...] if the boy had had the advantage of some athletic sport, he would doubtless have worked off most of the vague feelings which he mistook for the stirrings of genius' (Emeljanow, pp.139–40). A revival at the Comedy Theatre, New York, in April 1929, directed by someone with Moscow Art Theatre experience, Leo Bulgakov, struck the critic Brooks Atkinson as 'a work of unalloyed genius, and superior in the range of its story to *The Cherry Orchard* and *Three Sisters*' (Emeljanow, p.344). The 1970s saw five major restagings of *The Seagull* in New York alone, among the most interesting of which were 'avant-garde' versions by Andre Gregory and Joseph Chaikin. Working from a literal translation by Laurence Senelick, Gregory's actors reformulated the dialogue, paraphrasing the speeches, and replacing Dorn's snatches of romantic ballads with quotations from pop hits (Senelick: 1997, p.293). Chaikin's production, which was designed to be a 'confrontation between the old and the new, the conventional and the experimental', turned out to be 'traditional, deferential and dull' but drew plaudits from those critics who had tended to be disdainful of Gregory (ibid., pp.294–5). The English director, Ron Daniels, staged a production at the American Repertory Theatre, Cambridge,

Massachusetts, in 1989, alternating *The Seagull* with *Hamlet*
and casting the same actors in the 'double' roles of Hamlet/
Konstantin, Arkadina/Gertrude, Trigorin/Claudius, Nina/
Ophelia. Costumes were more or less contemporary for *The
Seagull*, with the bright colours for the early acts reminiscent of
the Spanish painter Joán Miró, but the setting for Act Four
was, by contrast, bare and black. In the spirit of the sexually
liberated times when nudity on stage was *de rigueur*, Daniels
had Arkadina strip to the waist in Act Two 'to display her
girlish attributes' (ibid., pp.300–1).

Mike Nichols staged *The Seagull* at the Delacorte Theatre in
New York's Central Park in 2001 with Meryl Streep as
Arkadina and Kevin Kline as Trigorin using Tom Stoppard's
version of the play. The production was notable for Streep's
cartwheels performed at the beginning of Act Two to illustrate
her youthfulness and for Konstantin's on-stage suicide but was
up-staged by a fringe production which opened simultaneously
at the Table and Chair Handmade Theatre of Karen Sunde's
Please God No Wedding or Shooting at the End. The play
imagines Chekhov returning home to write a review of a
production of *Hamlet* he has just seen which then turns into
his own play, *The Seagull*, in which Hamlet features alongside
Konstantin, Polonius counsels both Nina and Ophelia,
Konstantin complains to Hamlet about his own mother and
Hamlet and Claudius comment on Trigorin, whose life seems to
echo that of Chekhov himself, complete with Lika Mizinova
and Levitan's suicide attempt. When Masha complains to
Chekhov, 'I think you're writing *Hamlet*', the latter protests
that he's writing about writing with, please God, no wedding
or shooting at the end ... (*Plays International*, September
2001).

Further Reading

Bibliography (of primary sources referred to in the Commentary)

Allen, David, *Performing Chekhov* (London: Routledge, 2000)

Balukhaty, S.D. (ed. and intro.), *'The Seagull' Produced by Stanislavsky. Production Score for the Moscow Art Theatre*, trans. D. Magarshack (London: Dennis Dobson, 1952)

Barricelli, Jean-Pierre (ed.), *Chekhov's Great Plays: A Critical Anthology* (New York and London: New York University Press, 1981)

Bristow, Eugene K. (trans. & ed.), *Anton Chekhov's Plays* (New York: W.W. Norton & Co., 1977)

Clayton, J. Douglas (ed.), *Chekhov Then and Now: The Reception of Chekhov in World Culture* (New York: Peter Lang, 1997)

Emeljanow, Victor, *Chekhov: The Critical Heritage* (London: Routledge & Kegan Paul, 1981)

Gilman, Richard, *Chekhov's Plays: An Opening Into Eternity* (New Haven and London: Yale University Press, 1995)

Goriacheva M.O., A.P. Chudakov et al (eds), *Chekhoviana: Chekhov i serebriannyi vek* (Moscow: Nauka, 1996)

Gottlieb, Vera, *Chekhov in Performance in Russia and Soviet Russia* (Cambridge and Teaneck, NJ: Chadwick-Healey, 1984)

Gottlieb, Vera and Allain, Paul (eds), *The Cambridge Companion to Chekhov* (Cambridge: CUP, 2000)

Henry, Peter (ed.), A.P. Chekhov, *Chaika (The Seagull)* (Letchworth: Bradda Books, 1965; rev.ed., London: Bristol Classical Press, 1993)

Kuzicheva, A.P., *A.P. Chekhov v russkoi teatral'noi kritike: Kommentirovannaia antologiia 1887–1917*, (Moscow: Chekhovskii poligraficheskii kombinat, 1999)

Magarshack, David, *Chekhov the Dramatist* (London: John Lehmann, 1952)

Miles, Patrick, *Chekhov on the British Stage 1909–1987*

(England: Sam & Sam, 1987)

Miles, Patrick (ed.), *Chekhov on the British Stage* (Cambridge: CUP, 1993)

Peace, Richard, *Chekhov: A Study of the Four Major Plays* (New Haven and London: Yale University Press, 1983)

Pitcher, Harvey, *The Chekhov Play: A New Interpretation* (London: Chatto & Windus, 1973)

Rayfield, Donald, *Anton Chekhov: A Life* (New York: HarperCollins, 1997)

Rayfield, Donald, *Understanding Chekhov: A Critical Study of Chekhov's Prose and Drama* (London: Bristol Classical Press, 1999)

Senelick, Laurence, *Anton Chekhov* (London and Basingstoke: Macmillan, 1985)

Senelick, Laurence, *The Chekhov Theatre: A Century of the Plays in Performance* (Cambridge: CUP, 1997)

Styan, J.L., *Chekhov in Performance: A Commentary on the Major Plays* (Cambridge: CUP, 1971)

Valency, Maurice, *The Breaking String: The Plays of Anton Chekhov* (Oxford: OUP, 1966)

Additional material

Clyman, Toby W. (ed.), *A Chekhov Companion* (Westport and London: Greenwood Press, 1985)

Heim, M.H. (trans.) and Karlinsky, S. (commentary and intro.), *Letters of Anton Chekhov* (London: Bodley Head, 1973)

Jones, David Richard, *Great Directors at Work: Stanislavsky, Brecht, Kazan, Brook* (Berkeley: University of California, 1986)

Meister, Charles W., *Chekhov Bibliography: Works in English by and about Anton Chekhov; American, British and Canadian Performances* (Jefferson and London: McFarland & Co., 1985)

Williams, Raymond, *Drama in Performance* (Harmondsworth: Pelican Books, 1972)

Translator's Introduction

'A comedy – three f., six m., four acts, rural scenery (a view over a lake); much talk of literature, little action, five bushels of love.'

Chekhov's own synopsis of the play, in a letter to his friend Suvorin written a month before he finished it, is characteristically self-mocking and offhand. (His cast list is even one f. short, unless he added the fourth woman only during that last month, or when he revised the play the following year.) He says in the same letter that he is cheating against the conventions of the theatre, but no one could have begun to guess from his flippant résumé how extraordinary an event was being prepared for the world. No doubt Chekhov took the play more seriously than the letter suggests, but even he can scarcely have realised quite what he had on his hands: a catastrophe so grotesque that it made him swear never to write for the theatre again; a triumph so spectacular that it established him as a kind of theatrical saint; and the first of the four masterpieces that would change forever the nature and possibilities of drama.

Chekhov wrote *The Seagull* in 1895. He was 35 years old, and already an established and celebrated writer who had known almost nothing but success. But the success was on the printed page, as a writer of short stories, and the leap he was trying to make now, from page to stage, was one which few major writers have managed. He had written for the theatre before, of course. He had done a number of short plays, all but one broadly comic, and related to his humorous journalism rather than to his more serious work. He had also written at least three full-length plays with more serious intentions – the untitled piece of his student days, *Ivanov*, and *The Wood Demon* – and with these he had encountered almost the only setbacks of his career so far. Now, as he finished *The Seagull* and read it through, he had a moment of fundamental doubt about the direction he was trying to take. 'I am once again convinced,' he wrote to Suvorin, 'that I am absolutely not a dramatist.'

There were prolonged difficulties in getting the play past the theatrical censor (see A Note on the Translation), which almost made him despair of the whole enterprise, but once this hurdle was behind him Chekhov's apparently offhand mood returned. The play was to be performed at the Alexandrinsky Theatre in St Petersburg, where *Ivanov* had been well received seven years earlier after a highly disputed opening in Moscow, and his letters in September 1896, as rehearsals approached, have the same cheerful flippancy as his original account of the play to Suvorin. They read with hindsight as ironically as the banter of some doomed statesman as he goes all unknowning towards his assassination. To his brother Georgi: 'My play will be done in the Alexandrinsky Theatre at a jubilee benefit [for the actress Levkeyeva]. It will be a resounding gala occasion. Do come!' To his friend Shcheglov: 'Around the 6th [of October] the thirst for glory will draw me to the Palmyra of the north for the rehearsals of my *Seagull*.' To his brother Alexander: 'You are to meet me at the station, in full parade uniform (as laid down for a customs officer retd.) . . . On the 17th Oct my new play is being done at the Alexandrinsky. I would tell you what it's called, only I'm afraid you'll go around boasting you wrote it.'

The seventeenth, when it came, was indeed a resounding gala occasion. 'I have been going to the theatre in St Petersburg for more than twenty years,' wrote a correspondent in a theatrical journal afterwards, 'and I have witnessed a great many "flops" . . . but I can remember nothing resembling what happened in the auditorium at Levkeyeva's 25th jubilee.' The trouble started within the first few minutes of Act One. Levkeyeva was a popular light comedy actress, and even though she had no part in the play the audience were minded to laugh. The first thing that struck them as funny was the sight of Masha offering a pinch of snuff to Medvedenko, and thereafter they laughed at everything. Konstantin's play, Konstantin with his head bandaged – it was all irresistible. By Act Two, according to the papers next day, the dialogue was beginning to be drowned by the noise and movement of the audience; by Act Three the hissing had become general and deafening. The reviewers struggled for superlatives to describe 'the grandiose scale' of the play's failure, the 'scandalous' and 'unprecedented' nature of 'such a dizzying flop, such a stunning fiasco'. The author, they reported, had fled from the theatre.

According to his own accounts of the evening Chekhov escaped from the theatre only when the play ended, after sitting out two or three acts in Levkeyeva's dressing-room, had supper at Romanov's, 'in the proper way', then slept soundly and caught the train home to Melikhovo next day. Even Suvorin accused him of cowardice in running away. All he had run away from, he protested in a letter to Suvorin's wife, was the intolerable sympathy of his friends. He told Suvorin: 'I behaved as reasonably and coolly as a man who has proposed and been refused, and who has no choice but to go away ... Back in my own home I took a dose of castor oil, had a wash in cold water – and now I could sit down and write a new play.'

But Suvorin, with whom he was staying, recorded in his diary that Chekhov's first reaction had been to give up the theatre. He had not come back until two in the morning, when he told Suvorin that he had been walking about the streets, and that 'if I live another seven hundred years I shan't have a single play put on. Enough is enough. In this area I am a failure.' When he went home next day he left a note telling Suvorin to halt the printing of his plays, and saying that he would never forget the previous evening. He claimed to have slept well, and to be leaving 'in an absolutely tolerable frame of mind'; but he managed nevertheless to leave his dressing-gown and other belongings on the train, and the accounts he subsequently gave of the evening in various letters to friends and relations make it clear how painful the experience had been. 'The moral of all this', he wrote to his sister Masha, 'is that one shouldn't write plays.'

And yet, not much more than a month later, in another letter to Suvorin, he was mentioning the existence of a play 'not known to anyone in the world' – *Uncle Vanya*. By this time, too – in fact from the very next performance – the tide had turned at the Alexandrinsky. 'A total and unanimous success,' wrote Komissarzhevskaya, who was playing Nina, in a letter to

Chekhov after the second performance of *The Seagull*, 'such as it ought to be and could not but be.' And two years later, in a stunning reversal of fortune of the kind that occurs in plays (though never in Chekhov's own), it triumphed in Moscow as noisily as it had failed in Petersburg.

In fact the event went rather beyond anything one might find in a play; it was more like something out of a backstage musical – particularly as recounted by Stanislavsky (who was both directing and playing Trigorin) in his memoir of Chekhov. For a start the fate of the newly-founded Moscow Arts Theatre depended upon it. The other opening productions had mostly either failed or been banned by the Metropolitan of Moscow, and all hopes were now riding aboard this one salvaged wreck. There was a suitable love interest depending upon the outcome of the evening – the leading lady (Olga Knipper, playing Arkadina) and the author had just met, and were to marry two plays later – provided there *were* two more plays to allow their acquaintance to develop. Moreover, the author had now been diagnosed as consumptive and exiled to Yalta. The dress rehearsal was of course a disaster. At the end of it Chekhov's sister Masha arrived to express her horror at the prospect of what another failure like Petersburg would do to her sick brother, and they considered abandoning the production and closing the theatre.

When the curtain finally went up on the first night the audience was sparse, and the cast all reeked of the valerian drops they had taken to tranquillise themselves. As they reach the end of Act One Stanislavsky's paragraphs become shorter and shorter:

> We had evidently flopped. The curtain came down in the silence of the tomb. The actors huddled fearfully together and listened to the audience.
>
> It was as quiet as the grave.
>
> Heads emerged from the wings as the stage staff listened as well.
>
> Silence.
>
> Someone started to cry. Knipper was holding back hysterical sobs. We went offstage in silence.
>
> At that moment the audience gave a kind of moan and burst

into applause. We rushed to take a curtain.

People say that we were standing on stage with our backs half-turned to the audience, that we had terror on our faces, that none of us thought to bow and that someone was even sitting down. We had evidently not taken in what had happened.

In the house the success was colossal; on stage it was like a second Easter. Everyone kissed everyone else, not excluding strangers who came bursting backstage. Someone went into hysterics. Many people, myself among them, danced a wild dance for joy and excitement.

The only person who remained completely calm seems to have been Chekhov himself, since he was 800 miles away in the Crimea. But when after Act Three the audience began to shout 'Author! Author!', as audiences do in this kind of script, and Nemirovich-Danchenko explained to them that the author was not present, they shouted 'Send a telegram!' In the event he was informed of his triumph not only by telegram, but in shoals of letters from everyone present. But, judging by how rarely he referred to it either beforehand or afterwards in his own letters from Yalta, he had kept this production at a distance emotionally as well as geographically, and the Moscow success was considerably more remote from him than the Petersburg failure.

There were of course external reasons for the play's extraordinarily different reception in the two capitals. The choice of Levkeyeva's benefit night in St Petersburg, on the one hand, and the fact that it had been produced there at nine days' notice; the thorough preparation in Moscow on the other hand, with twelve weeks' rehearsal. The Moscow audience may also have been impressed by the sheer weight of Stanislavsky's production. At the beginning of Act One, for example, his prompt copy notes: 'Glimmer of lantern, distant singing of drunk, distant howling of dog, croaking of frogs, cry of corncrake, intermittent strokes of distant church bell . . . summer lightning, barely audible far-off thunder . . .' – All this before the first two characters have even got on stage. Chekhov, grateful as he was for the success, was ungratefully cool about the production when he finally saw it. He greatly

disliked the slowness of Stanislavky's tempo, and according to
Nemirovich-Danchenko he threatened to put a stage-direction in
his next play saying: 'The action takes place in a country where
there are no mosquitoes or crickets or other insects that
interfere with people's conversations.'

Even without Levkeyeva or the corncrakes, though, the play
would almost certainly have elicited a passionate response of
one kind or another. Its influence has been so widespread and
pervasive since that it is difficult now to realise what a
departure it was. The traditional function of literature in
general, and of drama in particular, has always been to simplify
and formalise the confused world of our experience; to isolate
particular emotions and states of mind from the flux of feeling
in which we live; to make our conflicts coherent; to illustrate
values and to impose a moral (and therefore human) order
upon a non-moral and inhuman universe; to make intention
visible, and to suggest the process by which it takes effect. *The
Seagull* is a critical survey of this function. For a start two of
the characters are writers. One of them is using the traditional
techniques without questioning them, one of them is searching
for some even more formalised means of expression; and what
interests Chekhov is how life eludes the efforts of both of them.
Konstantin cannot even begin to capture it, for all the
seriousness of his intentions; Trigorin feels that in the end all
he has ever managed to do without falsity is landscapes, while
his obsessive need to write drains his experience of all meaning
apart from its literary possibilities. The extraordinary trick of
the play is that all around the two writers we see the very life
that they fail to capture. What Chekhov is doing, in fact, is
something formally impossible – to look behind the
simplification and formalisation by which the world is
represented in art and to show the raw, confused flux of the
world itself, where nothing has its moral value written upon it,
or for that matter its cause or its effect, or even its boundaries
or its identity.

The most obvious characteristic of this approach is the play's
ambiguity of tone. The author does not give us any of the
customary indications as to whether we are to find these events
comic or tragic. Indeed, what we are watching has not been

clearly organised into *events*; a lot of it bears a striking
resemblance to the non-events out of which the greater part of
our life consists. Then again, the play is to a quite astonishing
extent morally neutral. It displays no moral conflict and takes
up no moral attitude to its characters. Even now, after all these
years, some people still find this difficult to accept. They talk as
if Arkadina and Trigorin, at any rate, were monsters, and as
if the point of the play were to expose her egotism and his
spinelessness. It is indeed impossible not to be appalled by
Arkadina's insensitivity towards her son, or by the ruthlessness
with which she attempts to keep Trigorin attached to her;
moral neutrality is not moral blindness. But Konstantin
continues to find good in her, for all his jealousy and irritation,
and she remains capable of inspiring the love of those around
her. Konstantin's assessment is just as valid as ours; the
devotion of Dorn and Shamrayev is just as real and just as
important as our outrage. There is moral irony, too, in her
manipulation of Trigorin; had she succeeded more completely in
blackmailing him to remain with her she might have saved
Nina from the misery that engulfs her. It is hard to respect
Trigorin as we see him crumble in Arkadina's hands, harder
still to like him when we know how he has treated Nina. But
Masha likes and respects him, and for good reason – because
he listens to her and takes her seriously; no grounds are offered
for discounting her judgement. And when Trigorin wanders
back in the last act, makes his peace with Konstantin, and
settles down to lotto with the others, he is once again neither
good nor bad in their eyes, in spite of what he has done; he is
at that moment just a man who always seems to come out on
top, whether in lotto or in love. We are perfectly entitled to
find against him, of course – but that is our own verdict; there
has been no direction to the jury in the judge's summing-up;
indeed, no summing-up and no judge.

But then nothing is fixed. Everything is open to
interpretation. Are we, for instance, to take Konstantin
seriously as a writer? Impossible, after Nina's complaint that
there are no living creatures in his work. But then it turns out
that Dorn likes it, and he is a man of robust good sense
(though not good enough to prevent his ruining of Polina's

life). And in Act Four we discover that Konstantin is at any rate good enough to be able to make a career as a professional writer. But even then Trigorin's judgement remains the same as Nina's, and Konstantin comes round to much the same view himself.

No one is valued for us; nothing is firmly located or fully explained. Why is Arkadina called Arkadina? She is Sorina by birth and Trepleva by marriage. It could be a stage-name, of course, or she could have married more than once. The people around her presumably know. They do not trouble to tell us. Has Dorn had an affair with Arkadina in the past? Is this why Polina is so relentlessly jealous of her? Is it what Arkadina is referring to when she talks about how irresistible he had been in the past? (In an earlier draft Polina begins to weep quietly at this point; but that may of course be for the lost early days of her own love.) In an astonishing moment at the end of Act One we do in fact stumble across one of the unexplained secrets of this world, when Dorn snatches Masha's snuffbox away from her, admonishes her for her 'filthy habit', and flings it into the bushes. From that one gesture of licensed impatience, without a word being said, we understand why Masha feels nothing for her father, why she feels so close to Dorn; because Dorn is her father, not Shamrayev. But who knows this, apart from us and Dorn? Not Masha herself, apparently. Does Shamrayev? Arkadina? Medvedenko? We are not told; the clouds that have parted for a moment close in again.

But then which of them knows about Dorn's relationship with Masha's mother in the first place? Perhaps everyone; or perhaps no one. We can only speculate. In any case it is characteristic of the relationships in the play; overt or covert, they are all one-sided, unsatisfactory, anomalous, and unlikely ever to be resolved. Medvedenko loves Masha who loves Konstantin who loves Nina who loves Trigorin who is supposed to love Arkadina, but who doesn't really love anyone, not even himself. No one's life can be contained in the forms that marriage and family offer. Konstantin's dissatisfaction with the existing dramatic forms is only a special case of this general condition. Plainly Chekhov is not advocating new social forms, in the way that Konstantin is calling for new literary ones. In the end even Konstantin comes to think that it is not a question of forms, old or new – the important thing is to write from the heart; nor are there any social forms suggested in the play which could ever contain the great flux of life itself.

We cannot help wondering, of course, if in this play we for once catch a glimpse of its elusive author. Chekhov is astonishingly absent from his works. Even the most intimately understood of his characters is unlike him – from quite different backgrounds, most of them, with quite different feelings and outlooks. But here is a play about two professional writers; it must surely reflect his own experience in some way. Konstantin is scarcely a plausible candidate, overwhelmed as he is by an artistic family, obsessed by questions of literary theory, and unable to create a living character; Chekhov's parents, after all, ran a provincial grocery, he displayed no interest in theory, and life is the very quality in which his stories and plays abound. But Trigorin is another matter. He is a celebrated and successful author, in much the same way that Chekhov was. His passion is fishing; so was Chekhov's. His modest estimate of his place in Russian letters is very much the kind of thing that Chekhov might have said mockingly about himself. More importantly, it seems at any rate plausible that his painful memories of beginning his career, and the terrible compulsion to write which is eating his life, reflect something that Chekhov felt about himself – particularly since the only palliative for his obsession is fishing. But this is about as far as we can push the parallel. David Magarshack, in his book *The Real Chekhov*, goes on to suppose that Trigorin is Chekhov's spokesman, and that when he tells Nina about the need he feels to pronounce on social questions he is making some kind of declaration of social commitment on Chekhov's behalf. This is preposterous. Trigorin is not even issuing a manifesto on his own behalf – he is making a confession of helplessness and ineptitude. Chekhov was notorious for refusing to pronounce on social questions, and if there is any manifesto in *The Seagull* it is plainly its general orientation *against* the imposition of the author's own interpretations and views upon his material.

All autobiographical parallel has in any case clearly broken down by this point. There would be something characteristically self-mocking in choosing a second-rate author to represent himself, but when Trigorin says finally that all he can write is landscapes we realise that the picture which has been built up deliberately excludes the very essence of Chekhov's literary identity. Nor do any of the other biographical details fit. Arkadina is indeed based in part upon an actress, Yavorkskaya, who seems from her letters to have been very briefly his mistress. But Chekhov, unlike Trigorin, had no difficulty in disentangling himself from her, and in keeping women at arm's length generally. One of the women who were in love with Chekhov, Lika Mizinova, he kept at bay so successfully that she provided a model for not one but two of the characters in *The Seagull*: first Masha, with her life ruined by the unquenchable but unreciprocated love she has for Konstantin, and then Nina. To forget the Masha-like feelings she had for Chekhov, Lika threw herself into a disastrous affair with a friend of his, the Ukrainian writer Potapenko, who left his wife and went off to Paris with Lika, where he made her pregnant and then abandoned her. Potapenko, ironically, having provided Chekhov with a model for the more dubious aspects of Trigorin, was then called upon by him, after the play was finished, to undertake all the endless negotiations with the censor for him.

Nina was also contributed to by another of Chekhov's admirers, the writer Lidia Avilova, whom he treated even more high-handedly. She gave him a charm for his watch-chain with a page reference inscribed upon it, exactly as Nina does Trigorin with the medallion, and referring to a passage in one of Chekhov's stories which is exactly the same as the passage in Trigorin's works referred to by Nina's present – 'If ever you have need of my life, then come and take it'. Meeting her later at a masked ball, Chekhov promised to give her the answer to this from the stage in his new play. Ronald Hingley, in his biography of Chekhov, recounts how she went to the catastrophic first night in St Petersburg and struggled to hear the promised answer through the uproar all around her. She noted the page-reference given by Nina to locate the passage in Trigorin's works, and when she got home looked up the same page and line in a volume of her own stories. It read: 'Young ladies should not attend masked balls.' By this time, anyway, says Hingley, Chekhov had passed Avilova's fervently inscribed charm on to Komissarzhevskaya, the actress playing Nina, and it was being used on stage as a prop. If Chekhov had modelled Trigorin's behaviour with women on his own the play would have been deprived of Acts Three and Four.

It has to be recognised, I think, that there are some elements in the play which Chekhov has not completely succeeded in accommodating to his new aesthetic. Arkadina's aside after she believes she has broken Trigorin's will to leave her, 'Now he's mine,' (at any rate if played 'to herself', as written) seems to stem more from nineteenth-century dramatic convention than from life. Still, she is an actress by profession; it may be she rather than Chekhov who has imported the line from the theatre. Then again, Konstantin's account in Act Four of what has happened to Nina over the past two years seems to me awkwardly and belatedly expository, dramatically inert, and curiously old-fashioned in tone. Again, though, a similar justification might be offered – that it is only natural for Konstantin, as a writer of the time, to talk like a nineteenth-century short story. The soliloquies, too, seem to me a breach of the convention that Chekhov has established. If we are elsewhere left, as we are in life, to work out for ourselves what people are thinking and feeling from what they actually choose or happen to say to each other, why should we suddenly be given direct access, by means of a traditional stage convention, to Dorn's actual thoughts about Konstantin's play, or to Konstantin's assessment of his own stories? I was tempted to reorganise the scenes a little to avoid the need for soliloquy in Uncle Vanya, but by the time he came to write the last two plays he had abandoned it. The only apparent exception is Firs, locked into the house alone at the end of The Cherry Orchard. But he is not really soliloquising; he is an old man talking to himself, as he has earlier even in other people's presence.

These are small points. The other complaints which are sometimes made against the play seem to me to stem from misunderstandings. The symbolism, for instance, is occasionally disparaged as a portentous device to be outgrown by Chekhov

in the three later and even greater plays. There is in fact only
one piece of symbolism – though it recurs throughout the play
– and that is the motif of the seagull itself. Now for a start it
is not true that symbolic images of this sort do not occur in the
last three plays. Moscow plainly stands for much more than its
geographical self in *Three Sisters*; so does Natasha's
colonisation of the Prozorovs' house; while the cherry orchard
and its destruction must be one of the most suggestive and
powerful symbols ever used on the stage. In the second place
the symbolism of the dead seagull is set up not by Chekhov
but by Konstantin, as Nina immediately recognises when he
lays the bird accusingly at her feet. It is part of the
portentousness and inertness of Konstantin's art, not of
Chekhov's – and it is then taken up by Trigorin and absorbed
into the machinery of *his*, when he discovers the dead bird and
outlines his story of the girl who is destroyed with the same
wilfulness and casualness. Between them they burden Nina with
an image for herself and her fate that comes to obsess her. One
of the themes of the play, as I have argued, is the way in
which art warps and destroys the life that it draws upon. The
message of the seagull, as it stands there stuffed and forgotten
at the end of the play, is precisely of the deadness of the
symbolic process.

Many people, too, have had difficulty in the past with the
scene in the last act between Nina and Konstantin. The
difficulty has arisen because it has often been regarded, and
played, as a version of the traditional mad scene, where the
pathos of the heroine who has lost or been rejected by her love
is demonstrated by her retreat from reality into a world of
illusion. This is plainly not the case with Nina for the greater
part of the scene; she gives an entirely clear, calm, and sane
account of her experiences. The problem comes when she says,
as she does in all the English translations of the play that I
have come across, 'I am a seagull.' The poor girl thinks she is
a bird; her mind is plainly going. Now, there is a much more
reasonable construction to place upon her words here – and if
there is a choice then a reasonable construction must surely
always be preferred in interpreting a character's behaviour –
but it is obscured by a difficulty in the translation of the

Russian that may at first sight seem quibblingly small. In the Russian language there is no such thing as an article, either definite or indefinite. No distinction can be made, in speech or thought, between what English-speakers are forced to regard as two separable concepts – 'a seagull' and 'the seagull'. So when Nina signs her letters '*Chaika*' (Seagull), it is perfectly open to Konstantin to regard this as a sign of distraction, of the sort suffered by the grief-stricken miller in Pushkin's *Rusalka*, who tells people he is a raven. But what Nina herself means, surely, when the distinction has to be made in English, is not that she is *a* seagull but that she is *the* seagull. In other words, she is not identifying with the bird but with the girl in Trigorin's story, who is the Seagull in the same way that Jenny Lind was the Swedish Nightingale, or Shakespeare was the Swan of Avon. This is the idea that has seized hold of her – not that she has white wings and a yellow beak – but that she has been reduced to the status of a manipulated character in Trigorin's fiction – a character whose fate can be summed up in a single image. This is an obsessive thought, and she makes repeated efforts to throw it off, but it is not in any sense a deluded one. She *has* been manipulated; she is another victim of the distorting and deadening process of art. One can't help wondering if Avilova and Lika Mizinova ever came to feel that they had this in common with Nina, as well as everything else.

If her picture of herself as being the seagull of Trigorin's projected story is sane and sober, so is her claim to have found her way at last as an actress. We have no way of judging whether her hopes are well-founded; but her feeling that she is on the right path at last is an entirely rational one. Konstantin takes it seriously, anyway – seriously enough to realise that he by comparison is still lost, and to shoot himself in despair as a result. Faced with that testimony to the seriousness of his judgement we are scarcely in a position to dissent.

And this in fact is the final irony of the play – that in the end the Seagull herself escapes, wounded but still flying. It is the shooter who is shot, the writer who is written to death. Konstantin, not Nina, turns out to be the real victim of Trigorin's story, the true Seagull; Konstantin, who first brought the creature down to earth and declared it to be a symbol, is the one who ends up symbolised, lying as inert and irrelevant in the next room as the poor stuffed bird is in this. Perhaps Mizinova and the others found some symbolic comfort in that.

MICHAEL FRAYN

A Note on the Translation

I have been more ruthless than ever with the names. In English translation, it seems to me, the characters all become native English-speakers, and native English-speakers do not attempt foreign words and names. They are particularly unlikely to start on the treacherous combination of given-name-plus-patronymic that occurs so often in Russian, and would indeed be ill-advised to try, except perhaps in extreme circumstances, such as attempting to get a table in a Moscow restaurant by claiming acquaintance with the head waiter. Few of the occasions in the play when names are used in the Russian have survived this stringent test.

There are a number of literary allusions in the play, most of them, fortunately from a translator's point of view, to Shakespeare, and clearly identified as such by the characters who make them. I have in fact added an extra line of Shakespeare. In the original, Arkadina slips into playing the closet scene from *Hamlet* with Konstantin because in Russian Gertrude's speech begins 'My son'. I have made her start with a line of Gertrude's from the play scene as an alternative way in. But there are one or two Russian allusions that should be mentioned. Sorin, in Act Three, goes into town to get away for a little from what he calls, in the original, 'this gudgeon's life'. I have slightly reorganised this to make it at any rate clear to non-anglers that gudgeons live in the mud on the river-bottom. But I can find no way to suggest the literary background of the allusion, which is to the fish in Saltykov-Shchedrin's chilling fable *The Wise Gudgeon*. Saltykov's gudgeon, terrified of being eaten by a pike or crushed by a crab, digs a hole in the mud and hides himself in it, only to emerge to snatch his food when everything else is asleep and then to rush back in terror, unable ever to fulfil his natural function in life by marrying and having children. 'And in this way', says Saltykov, 'the wise gudgeon lived a hundred years and more. And all the time he trembled

and he trembled. Neither friends nor relations did he have; he
neither went to see anyone nor did anyone come to see him.
He never played cards, nor drank strong drink, nor smoked
tobacco, nor chased after pretty girls – only trembled and
thought the one same thought: "God be praised, I seem to be
alive!"' This is the picture of Sorin's life that the original would
suggest to a Russian audience. The danger that terrifies the
poor gudgeon most, incidentally, is the prospect of being caught
by an angler and turned into fish-soup – a fate which Sorin
avoided but which one might think Nina did not.

Konstantin, in Act Four, refers to the mad miller in *Rusalka*.
This is the fragment of a verse-drama by Pushkin about a
miller's daughter who is made pregnant and abandoned by a
prince. She throws herself into the millstream, whereupon her
father becomes demented with grief, and declares that he is the
raven of the locality. The drowned girl herself becomes a
rusalka, a water-spirit like a mermaid, and seems to be on the
point of getting her revenge when the fragment ends. The
parallel with Nina and Trigorin is obvious.

There is another quotation, or what appears to be a
quotation, that I have not been able to identify. Arkadina's line
in Act One, given here as 'Come, then, away, ill-starred old
man', appears in Russian to be metrical in form and poetic in
vocabulary and word-order. I assume it is a line from some
part which Arkadina has played, and indeed in an earlier draft
of the act she goes on to add: 'In some play or other it says:
"Come to your senses, old man!"' Arkadina's line in Act Two,
given here as 'I am troubled in my soul', also looks suspiciously
poetic in the original. I have consulted a number of sources and
a number of Russian friends without success. The lines may
well be from forgotten plays, or even entirely fictitious. On the
other hand there may be a little more meaning to be gleaned
here.

Chekhov gives precise references for all the songs that Sorin
and Dorn sing to themselves. I have retained the titles of only
the two which may still be familiar. The others, which have
disappeared into the mists of time and would be entirely
unfamiliar even if disinterred from the archives, I have reduced
to unspecified humming. On the other hand I have slightly

expanded Dorn's reference to Jupiter's anger in Act One to reconstruct the classical saying to which it alludes.

I have followed the new and authoritative 30-volume *Complete Collected Works and Letters* in restoring the cuts and changes demanded by the censor. Potapenko, the friend who was ironically (see Introduction, p. lxxxviii) charged with shepherding the text through the process of censorship, reported to Chekhov that there were unexpected difficulties. 'Your Decadent looks with indifference upon his mother's love affairs, which is not allowed by the censor's rules.' The censor himself later wrote to Chekhov direct to remove all doubt about what he wanted done. 'I have marked a number of places in blue pencil,' he explained, 'in addition to which I think I should make clear that I had in mind not so much the expressions themselves as the general sense of the relations established by these expressions. The point is not the cohabitation of the actress and the writer, but the calm view taken of this state of affairs by her son and her brother.' Negotiations dragged on throughout the summer of 1896, with Chekhov making some changes and Potapenko making others. After one suggested alteration, in a letter to Potapenko, Chekhov added in exasperation: 'Or whatever you like, even a text from the Talmud.' In the first printed text of the play, in journal form in December 1896, which was not subject to theatrical censorship, Chekhov reverted to his original text. It is true that in all the subsequent book editions he used the censored text; but these were published with the assurance on the title-page that the plays they contained had been 'passed unconditionally by the censorship for production'. The changes are small and of no very great significance, but there seems no possible reason now for not using the text that Chekhov himself plainly wanted.

There is a double irony, as things turned out, in Konstantin's allusion to the censorship in the first act – one intended by Konstantin and another added by circumstance. I have slightly expanded the reference, to make it comprehensible while leaving it oblique (Russian audiences, of course, have more experience in reading between the lines). Konstantin explains his premature departure from university by likening himself to an item which has failed to appear in the press 'owing to circumstances beyond the editor's control'. Chekhov had the same difficulty with Trofimov in *The Cherry Orchard* – how to explain that someone had been expelled from university for his political activities. It was impossible to get a direct reference to this past the censor – but not, apparently, a reference to the process of censorship itself.

M.F.

Pronunciation of the Names

The following is an approximate practical guide. In general, all stressed 'a's are pronounced as in 'far' (the sound is indicated below by 'aa') and all stressed 'o's as in 'more' (they are written below as 'aw'). All unstressed 'a's and 'o's are thrown away and slurred. The 'u's are pronounced as in 'crude'; they are shown below as 'oo'. A 'y' at the beginning of a syllable, in front of another vowel, is pronounced as a consonant (i.e. as in 'yellow', not as in 'sky').

The characters:

Aar*kaar*deena (I*reen*a)
Konstan*teen* (*Kawst*ya)
*Saw*reen (Pe*troosh*a)
*Neen*a
Sham-*rye*-yev
Po*leen*a
*Maash*a
Tri*gaw*reen (Bo*rees* Aleks*ay*eveech)
Dawrn (Yev*gay*ni)
Medved*yenk*o (Sem*yawn*)
*Yaak*ov

Other names occuring in the play, in alphabetical order:

Chadin, Pashka – *Chaad*een, *Paash*ka
Gogol – *Gawg*ol
Grokholsky – Grok*hawl*sky
Izmailov – Iz-*my*-lov
Kharkov – *Khaar*kov
Krechinsky – Kre*cheen*sky
Mama – *Maam*a
Matryona – Matr*yawn*a
Molchanovka – Mol*chaan*ovka

Nekrasov – Ne*kraas*sov
Odessa – O*dyess*a
Papa – *Paap*a
Poltava – Pol*taav*a
Sadovsky – Sa*dawv*sky
Silva – *Seel*va
Slavyansky Bazar – Sla*vyan*sky Ba*zaar*
Suzdaltzev – *Soo*zdaltzev
Tolstoy – Tol*stoy*
Turgenyev – Toor-*gain*-yev
Yeletz – Ye*letz*
Yevgeni – Yev*gain*i

The Seagull

This translation of *The Seagull* was first performed at the Palace Theatre, Watford, on 7 November 1986, with the following cast:

ARKADINA, *an actress*	Prunella Scales
KONSTANTIN, *her son*	Lorcan Cranitch
SORIN, *her brother*	Antony Brown
NINA, *the young daughter of a wealthy landowner*	Irina Brook
SHAMRAYEV, *a retired lieutenant, Sorin's steward*	Donald Morley
POLINA, *his wife*	Jan Carey
MASHA, *his daughter*	Ingrid Craigie
TRIGORIN, *a novelist*	Paul Shelley
DORN, *a doctor*	Denys Hawthorne
MEDVEDENKO, *a teacher*	Tim Preece
YAKOV, *a workman*	Stephen Gray
SERVANTS	Ian Connaghan
	Ewan MacKinnon
A MAID	Emma Bingham

The action takes place on Sorin's country estate.
Between Acts Three and Four two years have elapsed.

Act One

A section of the park on SORIN's *estate. A broad avenue leads away from the audience into the depths of the park towards the lake. The avenue is closed off by a stage which has been hurriedly run up for some home entertainment, so that the lake is completely invisible. Right and left of the stage is a shrubbery. A few chairs and a garden table.*

The sun has just set. On the improvised stage, behind the lowered curtain, are YAKOV *and other* WORKMEN; *coughing and banging can be heard.* MASHA *and* MEDVEDENKO *enter left, on their way back from a walk.*

MEDVEDENKO. Why do you always wear black?

MASHA. I'm in mourning for my life. I'm unhappy.

MEDVEDENKO. Why? (*Reflectively.*) I don't understand. You've got your health. Your father may not be rich, but he's not badly off. I have a much harder time than you. I get 23 rubles a month all told – less deductions for the pension – and I don't go round in mourning.

> *They sit.*

MASHA. It's not a question of money. Even a beggar can be happy.

MEDVEDENKO. Theoretically. In practice it comes down to this: my mother and I, plus my two sisters and my little brother – and only 23 rubles a month coming in. You mean we don't have to eat and drink? There's no need for tea and sugar? No need for tobacco? I don't know how to manage.

MASHA (*looking round at the improvised stage*). The show will be starting soon.

MEDVEDENKO. Yes. A play written by Konstantin, and his

Nina will be acting in it. Two people in love, and today their souls will merge as they strive to create a single artistic impression. Whereas my soul and yours have no point of contact. I love you – I can't stay at home I long to see you so much – I walk three miles here and three miles back every day – and all I get from you is indifference. Well, it's understandable. I've no money – I've a large family . . . Who wants to marry a man who can't even support himself?

MASHA. Oh, fiddle. (*Takes a pinch of snuff.*) I'm very touched that you love me, but I can't say the same in return, and that's all there is to it. (*Offers him the snuffbox.*) Have a pinch.

MEDVEDENKO. Not for me.

Pause.

MASHA. So close. We'll probably have a storm during the night. If you're not philosophising you're going on about money. You seem to think the worst thing that can happen to anyone is poverty, but I think it's a thousand times easier to go round in rags and beg your bread than it is to . . . Well, you wouldn't understand . . .

Enter, right, SORIN *and* KONSTANTIN.

SORIN (*leaning on a stick*). The thing with me, though, is that I somehow never feel quite up to the mark when I'm in the country. No question about it – I'll never get used to being here. Went to bed at ten last night and woke up at nine this morning feeling I'd slept for so long that my brain had stuck to my skull, etcetera, etcetera. (*Laughs.*) Then after dinner I dropped off again, and now I feel as if a horse and cart had gone over me. It's like being in a bad dream, when all's said and done . . .

KONSTANTIN. You're right – you ought to be living in town. (*Sees* MASHA *and* MEDVEDENKO.) Listen, you'll be called when it starts – you're not supposed to be here now. Go away, will you.

SORIN (*to* MASHA). And would you mind asking your father to
have the dog let loose? It howls otherwise. My sister was
awake all night again.

MASHA. You can talk to my father yourself – I'm not going to.
Spare me that, at any rate. (*To* MEDVEDENKO.) Come on,
then.

MEDVEDENKO (*to* KONSTANTIN). You'll let us know before
it starts, then.

Exeunt MASHA *and* MEDVEDENKO.

SORIN. So the dog will be howling all night again. It's a funny
thing – I've never been able to live as I please when I've been
in the country. In the old days I used to take a month's leave
and come here to relax, simple as that, but then they'd so
pester you with all kinds of nonsense that from the moment
you arrived you'd want to be away again . . . Now I'm
retired, though, there's nowhere else to go, when all's said
and done. Like it or lump it . . .

YAKOV (*to* KONSTANTIN). We're off for a swim, then.

KONSTANTIN. All right, but I want you standing by in ten
minutes time. (*Looks at his watch.*) Not long before it starts.

YAKOV. Sir.

Exit YAKOV.

KONSTANTIN (*glancing over the improvised stage*). Now how
about this for a theatre. Curtain at the front, wings at the
side – then nothing beyond but empty space. No scenery.
The back of the stage opening straight on to the lake and the
horizon. The curtain goes up at half-past eight precisely, as
the moon rises.

SORIN. Splendid.

KONSTANTIN. If Nina's late then of course the whole effect
will be ruined. She ought to be here by now. Her father and
stepmother keep guard over her – getting out of the house is

like escaping from prison. (*Adjusts his uncle's tie.*) Your hair
needs a comb through it – so does your beard. You could do
with a trim, couldn't you?

SORIN (*combing his beard*). It's the tragedy of my life. Even as
a young man I always looked as though I'd been at the bottle,
simple as that. Women never liked me. (*Sitting down.*) Why
is my sister out of sorts?

KONSTANTIN. Why? Because she's bored. (*Sitting down beside
him.*) Because she's jealous. She's already set her mind against
me, and against having theatricals, and against my play, in
case her novelist takes a fancy to Nina. She doesn't know
anything about my play, but she already hates it.

SORIN (*laughs*). Oh, come, come . . .

KONSTANTIN. She's already vexed that in this one little theatre
it's Nina who will have the success, and not her. (*Looks at his
watch.*) A comic tale of human psychology, my mother.
Talented, unquestionably; intelligent, quite capable of being
moved by a book. Recite you the whole of Nekrasov by heart.
Ministers to the sick like an angel. But you try saying
something nice about Duse in her hearing! Oh dear me no!
She's the one who has to have the nice things said about her
and no one else, she's the one who has to be written about,
shouted about, admired for her extraordinary performance in
La Dame aux Camélias, or whatever; and because this drug
isn't available here in the country she gets bored and ill-
tempered, and all of us become her enemies – it's all our
fault. Then again she's superstitious – she's afraid of three
candles and the thirteenth of the month. She's mean with her
money. She's got seventy thousand rubles sitting in a bank
in Odessa – I know that for a fact. But ask her if you can
borrow some and she'll burst into tears.

SORIN. You've got it into your head that your mother doesn't
like your play, and you're working yourself up about it in
advance, simple as that. Calm down, now – your mother
worships you.

KONSTANTIN (*pulling the petals off a flower*). She loves me – she loves me not . . . She loves me – loves me not . . . Loves me – loves me not. (*Laughs.*) There you are – she doesn't love me. Well, of course she doesn't. She wants to live and love and dress in light colours, and there am I, twenty-five years old, perpetually reminding her that she's stopped being young. When I'm not there she's thirty-two – when I am she's forty-three; and that's why she hates me. Then again I don't acknowledge the theatre. She loves the theatre – she thinks she's serving humanity and the sacred cause of art, whereas in my view the modern theatre is an anthology of stereotypes and received ideas. When the curtain goes up, and there, in a room with three walls lit by artificial lighting because it's always evening, these great artists, these high priests in the temple of art, demonstrate how people eat and drink, how they love and walk about and wear their suits; when out of these banal scenes and trite words they attempt to extract a moral – some small and simple moral with a hundred household uses; when under a thousand different disguises they keep serving me up the same old thing, the same old thing, the same old thing – then I run and don't stop running, just as Maupassant ran from the sight of the Eiffel Tower, that weighed on his brain with its sheer vulgarity.

SORIN. We couldn't do without the theatre.

KONSTANTIN. What we need are new artistic forms. And if we don't get new forms it would be better if we had nothing at all. (*Looks at his watch.*) I love my mother, I love her deeply. But then she smokes, she drinks, she quite openly lives with that novelist, they're always bandying her name about in the papers – and I'm sick of it. Though sometimes what prompts me is just ordinary mortal egotism; I start to regret that my mother is a well-known actress, and I feel I should be happier if she were an ordinary woman. Uncle, what could be sillier or more hopeless than the position I've found myself in often enough: solid rows of celebrities sitting in her drawing-room, artists and writers, and me the only one among them who's a nobody, being put up with purely because I'm her son. Who am I? What am I? I left university half-way through owing to circumstances beyond the editor's control, as the phrase goes; I've no talents; I've no money; while according to my passport I'm a shopkeeper, a Kiev shopkeeper. My father *did* come from Kiev, of course – he *was* from the shopkeeping classes – although he was also a well-known actor. So that when all those artists and writers in her drawing-room would turn their gracious attention upon me I had the impression that with every glance they were measuring the depth of my nonentity. I could guess what they were thinking, and the humiliation of it hurt . . .

SORIN. Speaking of writers, tell me, what sort of fellow is this novelist of hers? Difficult to make him out. He never says anything.

KONSTANTIN. He's intelligent, straightforward, a person of somewhat – shall we say? – melancholy disposition. A very decent sort of man. He's still well short of forty, but he's already famous and thoroughly jaded . . . These days he drinks nothing but beer and has no time for young people. If we're talking about his work then it's – how can I put it? – well, it's charming, it's clever . . but . . if you've read Tolstoy or Zola then you won't want to read Trigorin.

SORIN. Yes, but take me, now – I've a soft spot for literary men. Once upon a time there were two things I passionately wanted in life: I wanted to marry and I wanted to become a literary man, and I never managed either. So there we are. Nice to be even a minor literary man, when all's said and done.

KONSTANTIN (*listens*). I can hear footsteps . . . (*Embraces his uncle.*) I can't live without her . . . Even the sound of her footsteps is wonderful . . . I'm so happy I don't know what I'm doing!

Goes quickly across to meet NINA *as she enters.*

My enchantress, my dream . . .

NINA (*anxiously*). I'm not late . . . Tell me I'm not late . . .

KONSTANTIN (*kissing her hands*). No, no, no . . .

NINA. I've been worrying about it all day. I was so terrified! I was afraid my father wouldn't let me go . . . But he's just gone out with my stepmother. The sky red – the moon already starting to rise – and I kept whipping and whipping the horse. (*Laughs.*) I'm glad, though. (*Firmly presses* SORIN'S *hand.*)

SORIN (*laughs*). We've been crying, haven't we . . . We can't have that, now.

NINA. It's nothing . . . Look how out of breath I am. I'm going in half-an-hour, we must hurry. You mustn't, mustn't, for heaven's sake, make me late. My father doesn't know I'm here.

KONSTANTIN. It's time to start, in any case. We must go and call everyone.

SORIN. I'll do it. Right away, simple as that. (*Goes off right, singing Schumann's 'Two Grenadiers', then looks round.*) I started singing like that once, and one of the deputy prosecutors looked at me and said: 'You know, sir, you have a very powerful voice.' Then he thought for a moment and he added: 'Very powerful, but very disagreeable.' (*Laughs and goes off.*)

NINA. My father and his wife won't let me come here. They say you're all Bohemians . . . They're afraid I might run off to be an actress . . . But it's the lake that draws me here, like a seagull . . . My heart's full of you. (*Looks round.*)

KONSTANTIN. We're alone.

NINA. I think there's someone there . . .

   They kiss.

NINA. What sort of tree is that?

KONSTANTIN. Elm.

NINA. Why does it have such a dark colour?

KONSTANTIN. It's evening – everything looks dark. Don't go early, please don't.

NINA. I can't stay.

KONSTANTIN. Supposing I came to your house, Nina? I'll stand in the garden all night and look up at your window.

NINA. You can't – the watchman will see you. Treasure's not used to you yet – he'll bark.

KONSTANTIN. I love you.

NINA. Shh . . .

KONSTANTIN (*hearing footsteps*). Who's that? Is that you, Yakov?

YAKOV (*behind the improvised stage*). Sir.

KONSTANTIN. Stand by. Time to start. Is the moon rising?

YAKOV. Sir.

KONSTANTIN. Have you got the spirits? And the sulphur? When the red eyes appear there must be a smell of sulphur. (*To* NINA.) Go on, then, it's all ready. Are you nervous?

NINA. Yes, very. I don't mind your mother, I'm not afraid of her, but you've got Trigorin here . . . When I think of acting in front of him I'm terrified, I'm ashamed . . . He's a famous writer . . . Is he young?

KONSTANTIN. Yes, he is.

NINA. Such wonderful stories he writes!

KONSTANTIN (*coldly*). I wouldn't know. I haven't read them.

NINA. Your play's so difficult to do. It doesn't have any living characters.

KONSTANTIN. Living characters! The point is not to show life the way it is, or the way it ought to be, but the way it comes to you in dreams.

NINA. It doesn't have much action, your play – it's just a kind of recitation. And I think a play absolutely has to have love in it . . .

They both go behind the improvised stage. Enter POLINA *and* DORN.

POLINA. It's getting damp. Go back and put your galoshes on.

DORN. I'm hot.

POLINA. You won't look after yourself. It's just pig-headedness. You're a doctor – you know perfectly well that dampness in the air is bad for you, but no, you want to make me suffer. Last night you sat out on the verandah all evening just to spite me . . .

> DORN *hums*.

You were so wrapped up in your conversation with *her* – you never noticed the cold. Admit it, now – you're fond of her.

DORN. I'm fifty-five.

POLINA. Oh, fiddle, that's not old for a man. You're perfectly well preserved and you're still attractive to women.

DORN. So what do you want me to do?

POLINA. You'll all bow down in front of an actress. Not one of you who won't!

DORN (*hums*). If artists are popular people, if they get treated differently from – what shall we say? – from businessmen, then that's the way the world's made. That's our yearning for higher things.

POLINA. You've always had women falling in love with you and hanging round your neck. Is that supposed to be a yearning for higher things?

DORN (*shrugs*). If you like. There's been much that was good in the relationships women have had with me. What they liked most about me was the fact I was a first-class doctor. Ten years or so back, you may recall, I was the only one in the whole province who could deliver a baby decently. Added to which I was always a man of honour.

POLINA (*seizes his hand*). Oh, my dear!

DORN. Hush, now. They're coming.

> *Enter* ARKADINA *on* SORIN's *arm*, TRIGORIN, SHAMRAYEV, MEDVEDENKO, *and* MASHA.

SHAMRAYEV. In 1873, at Poltava during the Fair, she gave an amazing performance. Sheer delight! A wonderful performance! And do you know where Chadin is these days, the comic actor? In *Krechinsky's Wedding* there was no one to touch him – he was better than Sadovsky, I promise you, dear lady. Where is he these days?

ARKADINA. You keep asking me about people who came out of the Ark! How should I know? (*Sits.*)

SHAMRAYEV (*sighs*). Pashka Chadin! They don't make them like that any more. The theatre's not what it was. Once there were mighty oaks – now we see mere stumps.

DORN. There's not much in the way of brilliant talent these days, it's true, but your average actor is of a much higher standard.

SHAMRAYEV. I can't agree. Though it's all a question of taste. *De gustibus aut bene aut nihil.*

KONSTANTIN *comes out from behind the improvised stage.*

ARKADINA (*to* KONSTANTIN). 'Come hither, my dear Hamlet, sit by me . . .' My precious, when's it going to begin?

KONSTANTIN. In a minute. If you would just be patient.

ARKADINA. 'O Hamlet, speak no more:
Thou turn'st mine eyes into my very soul;
And there I see such black and grained spots
As will not leave their tinct.'

KONSTANTIN. 'Nay, but to live
In the rank sweat of an enseamed bed
Stew'd in corruption, honeying and making love
Over the nasty sty . . .'

A horn sounds behind the improvised stage.

Ladies and gentlemen, the performance is about to begin. Your attention, if you please. (*Pause.*) I'm going to start. (*Knocks with a stick and speaks in a loud voice.*) You honoured ancient shades that hover in the hours of night above this lake, make our eyes grow heavy, and let us dream of what will be in two hundred thousand years from now!

SORIN. In two hundred thousand years from now there won't be anything.

KONSTANTIN. Then let them show us this not-anything.

ARKADINA. Let them. We're fast asleep.

The curtain rises. The view over the lake is revealed, with the moon above the horizon and its reflection in the water. On a large stone sits NINA, *all in white.*

NINA. Men and lions, partridges and eagles, spiders, geese, and antlered stags, the unforthcoming fish that dwelt beneath the waters, starfish and creatures invisible to the naked eye; in short – all life, all life, all life, its dismal round concluded, has guttered out . . . Thousands of centuries have passed since any living creature walked the earth, and this poor moon in vain lights up her lantern. In the meadows the dawn cry of the crane is heard no more, and the May bugs are silent in the lime groves. Cold, cold, cold. Empty, empty, empty. Fearful, fearful, fearful. (*Pause.*) The bodies of all living creatures have fallen into dust, and Everlasting Matter has turned them into stones, into water, into clouds; while all their souls have merged into one. And this one universal world soul is me . . . me . . . In me are the souls of Alexander the Great, of Caesar, of Shakespeare, of Napoleon, and of the least of leeches. In me the consciousness of human beings has merged with the instincts of animals. All, all, all do I remember, and every life I live again in my own self.

Marsh-lights appear.

ARKADINA (*quietly*). A touch of the Decadent School here, I think.

KONSTANTIN (*pleading and reproachful*). Mama!

NINA. I am quite alone. Once in every hundred years I open my lips to speak, and my voice echoes cheerlessly through this

emptiness where no one listens . . . Even you, pale fires, are
not listening to me . . . In the late watches of the night you
are born from the rotting swamp, and wander the world till
dawn, yet without the power of thought or will, without a
flicker of life. For fear that life might appear to you, the
Father of Eternal Matter, who is the Devil, effects in you, as
he does in stones and water, a constant replacement of the
atoms, and you are in a state of continual flux. One thing
alone in the universe stays unchanging and constant – spirit
itself. (*Pause.*) Like a prisoner flung into some deep dry well
I have no knowledge of where I am or of what awaits me. All
I am allowed to know is that in this stubborn, bitter struggle
with the Devil, marshal of all material forces, I am fated to
be victor; and that matter and spirit will thereafter merge in
wondrous harmony to usher in the reign of Universal Will.
But that will come about only after long tens of thousands of
years, when moon and bright Sirius and earth alike will
gradually turn to dust . . .

*Pause. Two red spots appear against the background of the
lake.*

Here comes my mighty adversary, the Devil, now. I see his
fearful crimson eyes . . .

ARKADINA. There's a smell of sulphur. Is there supposed to
be?

KONSTANTIN. Yes.

ARKADINA (*laughs*). I see – it's an effect.

KONSTANTIN. Mama!

NINA. He pines for human company . . .

POLINA (*to* DORN). You've taken your hat off. Put it on –
you'll catch cold.

ARKADINA. He's taken it off to the Devil, the Father of Eternal
Matter.

KONSTANTIN (*out loud, losing his temper*). Right, the play's over! That's it! Curtain!

ARKADINA. What are you getting cross about?

KONSTANTIN. That's it! Curtain! Can we have the curtain, please? (*Stamps his foot.*) Curtain!

The curtain is lowered.

I'm sorry! I was forgetting that playwriting and acting are reserved for the chosen few. I've infringed their monopoly! It. . .I. . .

He tries to say something else, but then flaps his hand and goes off left.

ARKADINA. What's got into him?

SORIN. Irina, my dear girl, that really is no way to deal with youthful pride.

ARKADINA. Why, what did I say?

SORIN. You offended him.

ARKADINA. He told us himself beforehand – it was an amusing skit. That's how I took it – as a skit.

SORIN. All the same . . .

ARKADINA. Now it turns out to be some great work of art! Oh, for heaven's sake! So he got up all this performance and perfumed the air with sulphur not to amuse us but to give us all an object-lesson in the art of writing and acting. Really, it's becoming a bore. These perpetual attacks on me, this campaign of pinpricks – it would tax the patience of a saint! He's a wilful, difficult boy.

SORIN. He wanted to give you pleasure.

ARKADINA. Oh, really? But he didn't pick some normal kind of play to do it with, did he? – He made us sit through these weary poetic ravings. For the sake of amusement I'm prepared to sit through even the ravings of delirium, but what we had here, I take it, were pretensions to new theatrical forms, to a new artistic era. So far as I could see, though, we didn't get new forms, we simply got bad manners.

TRIGORIN. Each of us writes as his fancy takes him and his talent allows.

ARKADINA. Let him write as his fancy takes him and his talent allows, just so long as he leaves me alone.

DORN. Jupiter wroth means Jupiter wrong.

ARKADINA. I'm not Jupiter – I'm a woman. (*Lights a cigarette.*) I'm not angry – I merely find it a bore that a young man should spend his time in such a tedious way. I didn't mean to offend him.

MEDVEDENKO. No one has any basis for separating spirit from matter, because for all we know spirit is nothing but the totality of material atoms. (*To* TRIGORIN, *with animation.*) But, you know, what someone ought to put in a play is how we teachers live. A hard, hard time we have of it!

ARKADINA. I'm sure you do, but let's not talk about either plays or atoms. Such a glorious evening! Listen, everyone – is that singing? (*Listens.*) How lovely!

POLINA. It's on the other side of the lake.

Pause.

ARKADINA (*to* TRIGORIN). Sit beside me. Ten years or so back on the lake here you could hear constant music and singing almost every night. There were six estates on this side. I remember laughter and noise and guns going off and everyone falling in love, falling in love . . . And the leading actor in all of this, the idol of all six estates, was . . . here he is – (*She nods at* DORN.) – the doctor. He's enchanting even now, but in those days he was irresistible. My conscience is beginning to prick, however. Why did I offend that poor boy of mine? I feel uneasy. (*Calls.*) Kostya! My son! Kostya!

MASHA. I'll go and look for him.

ARKADINA. Would you, my dear?

MASHA (*moving off left*). Halloo-oo! Halloo-oo!

She goes off. NINA *comes out from behind the improvised stage.*

NINA. We're obviously not going to do any more of it – I might as well come out. Hello.

She exchanges kisses with ARKADINA *and* POLINA.

SORIN. Bravo! Bravo!

ARKADINA. Bravo! Bravo! We all thought you were wonderful. With those looks, with that marvellous voice, you simply cannot stay lost in the depths of the countryside – it would be a sin. I'm sure you must have a talent. You hear? You absolutely must go on the stage!

NINA. Oh, that's my dream! (*Sighs.*) It will never come true, though.

ARKADINA. Who knows? Now, may I introduce: Trigorin – Boris Alekseyevich.

NINA. Oh, I'm so pleased to meet you . . . (*Overcome with embarrassment.*) I read everything you write . . .

ARKADINA (*sitting* NINA *down beside her*). Don't be embarrassed, my dear. He's a famous man, but he has a simple heart. You see – he's as embarrassed as you are.

DORN. I suggest they take the curtain up now. It's eerie like that.

SHAMRAYEV (*calls*). Yakov, take the curtain up, there's a good fellow!

The curtain goes up.

NINA (*to* TRIGORIN). It's a strange play, didn't you think?

TRIGORIN. I couldn't understand a word of it. I enjoyed watching it, though. You did it with such sincerity. And the scenery was lovely. (*Pause.*) There must be a lot of fish in that lake.

NINA. Yes, there are.

TRIGORIN. I love fishing. There's no greater pleasure I know than sitting on the bank at the end of the day and watching the float.

NINA. But I think that for anyone who has experienced the

pleasure of creating something all other pleasures must pale into insignificance.

ARKADINA (*laughing*). You mustn't talk like that. When people say nice things to him he just wishes the earth would swallow him up.

SHAMRAYEV. I remember an occasion at the Opera in Moscow when Silva, the famous bass, sang bottom C. Now that night, with malice aforethought, the bass from our church choir was sitting up in the gallery. Imagine our utter astonishment when suddenly we hear from the gallery, 'Bravo, Silva!' – a whole octave lower . . . Like this. (*In a deep but insubstantial bass.*) 'Bravo, Silva!' The whole theatre simply froze.

Pause.

DORN. A quiet angel flew past.

NINA. I must go. Goodbye.

ARKADINA. Go where? So early? We shan't let you.

NINA. Papa's waiting for me.

ARKADINA. Cruel man! Really . . .

They kiss.

Well, if you must you must. Such a shame to let you go.

NINA. If you knew how hard it is for me to leave!

ARKADINA. Someone ought to see you home, my pet.

NINA (*in alarm*). Oh, no, no!

SORIN (*pleading with her*). Do stay!

NINA. I really can't.

SORIN. Stay for one hour, simple as that. No harm, surely.

NINA (*on the verge of tears, after she has thought for a moment*). I mustn't! (*Presses his hand and quickly goes off.*)

ARKADINA. An unlucky girl, if truth be told. Apparently her late mother made all her huge wealth over to her husband – every last kopeck. Now the girl is left with nothing because her father in his turn has already made the whole lot over to his second wife. It's quite scandalous.

DORN. A real swine, though, her father, to give him his due.

SORIN (*rubbing his chilled hands*). We'd better be going, too, or it will get damp. My legs are aching.

ARKADINA. You look as if you've got a pair of wooden legs – you can scarcely walk on them. Come, then, away, ill-starred old man.

She takes his arm.

SHAMRAYEV (*offering* POLINA *his arm*). Madame?

SORIN. I can hear that dog howling again. (*To* SHAMRAYEV.) Be a good fellow, would you, and tell them to let it loose?

SHAMRAYEV. Can't be let loose, I regret to say. I'm afraid of thieves getting into the granary. I've got the millet in there. (*To* MEDVEDENKO, *who is walking beside him*.) Yes, a whole octave lower – 'Bravo, Silva!' And he wasn't an opera singer – just a simple member of the church choir.

MEDVEDENKO. What would someone in a church choir be paid?

Everyone except DORN *goes off.*

DORN (*alone*). Well, I don't know, I may be stupid, I may be mad, but I liked the play. There's something in it. When that little girl was talking about being on her own – and then when the Devil's red eyes appeared – I could feel my hands shaking with excitement. Something fresh and untutored about it . . . Here he comes, I think. I'd like to be a little nicer to him.

Enter KONSTANTIN.

KONSTANTIN. They've all gone.

DORN. I'm here.

KONSTANTIN. Masha's been looking all over the park for me. Intolerable woman.

DORN. Listen, I liked your play very much indeed. It was a strange kind of thing, and I didn't see the end of it, but it made a powerful impression none the less. You have talent; you must go on.

> KONSTANTIN *squeezes his hand hard and embraces him impetuously*.

So over-sensitive! Tears in your eyes . . . What was I going to say? Yes, you took a subject from the realm of abstract ideas. That was right, because a work of art must always express some substantial thought. Nothing can be excellent unless it be serious. You look quite pale!

KONSTANTIN. So you're saying – 'Go on'!

DORN. I am . . . But write about nothing that isn't important and eternal. I've lived my life with variety and taste, I'm a contented man, but I can tell you, if it had been granted to me to experience the lift of the heart that artists know in the moment of creation, then I think I should have scorned this material envelope of mine, and everything to do with it, and I should have left the ground and soared up into the heights.

KONSTANTIN. I'm sorry – where's Nina?

DORN. And another thing. In anything you write there must be a clear and definite thought. You must know why you're writing. If you don't, if you go down the picturesque path that has no definite goal at the end of it, then you'll lose your way, and your talent will destroy you.

KONSTANTIN (*impatiently*). Where's Nina?

DORN. She went home.

KONSTANTIN (*in despair*). What am I going to do? I want to see her . . . I have to see her . . . I'm going to go there . . .

> *Enter* MASHA.

DORN (*to* KONSTANTIN). Now, calm down, my friend.

KONSTANTIN. I'm going to go, all the same. I must go.

MASHA (*to* KONSTANTIN). Will you go into the house? Your mother's waiting. She's feeling uneasy about you.

KONSTANTIN. Tell her I've gone. And please, all of you, leave me alone! Just leave me alone! Don't follow me around!

DORN. Now, now, now, come on . . . Not the way . . . Not right.

KONSTANTIN (*on the verge of tears*). Goodbye, doctor. Thank you . . .

He goes off.

DORN (*sighs*). Youth, youth!

MASHA. Whenever there's nothing more to be said then people say: 'Youth, youth . . .' (*Takes a pinch of snuff.*)

DORN (*takes the snuffbox away from her and flings it into the bushes*). That's a filthy habit! (*Pause.*) I think they've started playing cards inside. I must go.

MASHA. Wait a moment.

DORN. What is it?

MASHA. Yet another thing I want to tell you. I'd like to talk for a moment . . . (*Becoming agitated.*) I don't like my father . . . but you have a special place in my heart. I don't know why, but all my life I've felt you were close to me . . . Help me. Please help me, or I shall do something silly – I shall make a mockery of my life, I shall ruin it . . . I can't go on . . .

DORN. What do you mean? Help you with what?

MASHA. I'm in such torment. No one knows, no one knows the torment I'm in! (*Lays her head on his breast; quietly.*) I'm in love with Konstantin.

DORN. You're all so over-sensitive! So over-sensitive! And so much love around . . . Oh, the spells woven by this lake! (*Tenderly.*) But what can I do, my child? What can I do?

CURTAIN

Act Two

The croquet lawn. In the distance to the right is the house, with a wide verandah, while to the left can be seen the lake, with the sun sparkling on it. Flower-beds and midday heat. At the side of the lawn, on a garden seat in the shade of an old lime-tree, are sitting ARKADINA, DORN, *and* MASHA. DORN *has a book open in his lap.*

ARKADINA (*to* MASHA). Both of us stand up.

> *They both stand.*

> Side by side. Now, you're twenty-two and I'm nearly twice that. Doctor, which of us is the younger-looking?

DORN. You are, of course.

ARKADINA. You see? And why? Because I work, I'm alive to the world around me, I'm always busy; whereas you're such a stick-in-the-mud, you don't know how to live . . . Also I make it a rule not to look into the future. I never think about old age, I never think about death. What will be, will be.

MASHA. Yes, but I feel as though I'd been born a long, long time ago; I'm dragging my life behind me like a dress with an endless train . . . And often I've no desire to go on living. (*Sits.*) Well, that's all nonsense, of course. You just have to shake yourself out of it.

> DORN *quietly sings Siebel's aria, 'Faites-lui mes aveux,' from Act III of Gounod's* Faust.

ARKADINA. Then again, my dear, I'm as careful about my appearance as an Englishman. I always keep myself firmly in hand. My dress, my hair – always *comme il faut*. Should I ever allow myself to go out of the house – even into the garden here – in a housecoat, or with my hair not done? Never. If I've kept my looks it's because I've never stopped caring about my appearance, I've never let myself go in the way that some women do . . . (*Walks about the lawn, hands on her hips.*) There you are, you see – spry as a kitten. I could play a girl of fifteen still.

DORN. Nonetheless and notwithstanding, I'm still reading, am I? (*Picks up the book.*) We stopped at the corn-chandler and the rats . . .

ARKADINA. And the rats, yes. Go on, then. (*Sits.*) Or rather, give it to me and I'll read. It's my turn. (*Takes the book and runs her eyes over it to find the place.*) The rats . . . Here we are . . . (*Reads.*) 'And, to be sure, it is as dangerous for people in society to make much of writers and to entice them into their homes as it would be for a corn-chandler to keep rats in his shop. And yet there is a vogue for them. So, when a woman has designs upon a writer whom she wishes to take up, she lays siege to him with compliments and attentions and little marks of favour . . . .' Well, that may be how it is with the French, but with us there's nothing like that – we don't work to a programme. Before a woman takes a writer up in this country she's usually head over heels in love with him, thank you very much. You don't have to look far – take me and Trigorin, for instance . . .

Enter SORIN, *leaning on his stick, with* NINA *beside him, and* MEDVEDENKO *pushing an empty wheelchair behind them.*

SORIN (*in the tone of voice used for being nice to a child*). So – we're all smiles, are we? We're all bright and cheerful today? (*To* ARKADINA.) We're all sunshine and smiles! Our father and stepmother have gone into town, and now we're as free as the air for three whole days.

NINA (*sits beside* ARKADINA *and embraces her*). I'm happy! I'm all yours now.

SORIN (*sits in his wheelchair*). As pretty as a picture she is today.

ARKADINA. Attractive, well turned out . . . What a sensible

girl. (*Kisses her.*) Still, we mustn't praise her too much or it will bring bad luck. Where's Trigorin?

NINA. He's at the bathing-place, fishing.

ARKADINA. You'd think he'd get bored with it. (*Resumes her book.*)

NINA. What are you reading?

ARKADINA. Maupassant, my sweet – *On the Water.* (*Reads a few lines to herself.*) Anyway, the next bit is neither amusing nor true. (*Shuts the book.*) I am troubled in my soul. Can anyone tell me what the matter is with my son? Why is he being so stern and boring? He spends whole days together on the lake – I scarcely see him.

MASHA. He's sick at heart. (*To* NINA, *shyly.*) Please – read a bit of his play!

NINA (*shrugs*). Do you really want me to? It's so dull!

MASHA (*restraining her enthusiasm*). When he reads something himself his eyes blaze and his face grows pale. He's got a wonderful sad voice; yes, and the manner of a poet.

SORIN *snores.*

DORN. Sleep well!

ARKADINA. Petrusha!

SORIN. Um?

ARKADINA. Are you asleep?

SORIN. Certainly not.

Pause.

ARKADINA. You're not having any medical attention, are you. It's not right.

SORIN. I'd be delighted to have some medical attention. It's the doctor here who won't give me any.

DORN. Medical attention? When you're sixty?

SORIN. Even when you're sixty you still want to live.

DORN (*irritably*). Tch! Well, take some valerian drops, then.

ARKADINA. I have a feeling it would be good for him to go to a spa somewhere.

DORN. All right. He could go to a spa. Or not go to a spa.

ARKADINA. Make sense of that, if you can!

DORN. There's nothing to make sense of. It's all perfectly plain.

Pause.

MEDVEDENKO. Your brother ought to give up smoking.

SORIN. Oh, fiddle.

DORN. No, not fiddle. Alcohol and tobacco make you lose the sense of yourself. Smoke a cigar or drink a glass of vodka and you're no longer you – you're you plus someone else. The self grows blurred, and you start to see yourself as a third person – not as 'I' but as 'he'.

SORIN (*laughs*). It's all very well for you to talk. You've lived in your time. But how about me? I spent twenty-eight years working in the Department of Justice, but I still haven't lived, when all's said and done, I still haven't experienced anything, and I long to live, no question about it. You've had your fill in life and you don't care any more, so you tend to be philosophical, but I want to live, and so I drink sherry at dinner and smoke cigars, it's as simple as that. As simple as that.

DORN. Life has to be taken seriously. Swallowing medicine when you're sixty and feeling sorry you didn't have much fun when you were young – forgive me if I'm blunt – but that's fatuous.

MASHA (*stands up*). It must be lunchtime. (*Walks limply and lethargically.*) My leg's gone to sleep . . . .

Exit MASHA.

DORN. Lunch . . . She's going to go and have a couple of drinks first.

SORIN. You can't expect a beggar to be happy.

DORN. Oh, pish, you old civil servant.

SORIN. You speak as someone who's had his fill in life.

ARKADINA. Oh, what could be more boring than this sweet country boredom! Heat, quiet, nothing anyone wants to do, everyone philosophising away . . . It's nice being with you, my friends, it's a pleasure to listen to you, and yet . . . to be sitting in a hotel room somewhere learning your lines – could anything be better than that?

NINA (*enthusiastically*). Oh, yes! I know what you mean.

SORIN. It's better in town, no doubt about it. You sit in your office, no one gets past the attendant without being announced, there's the telephone, there are cabs in the street – it's as simple as that . . .

DORN *sings* 'Faites-lui mes aveux . . .'

Enter SHAMRAYEV, *followed by* POLINA.

SHAMRAYEV. So this is where they are! A very good day to you all! (*Kisses* ARKADINA's *hand, then* NINA's.) Delighted to find you in good health. (*To* ARKADINA.) My wife tells me you're proposing to go into town together. Is this true?

ARKADINA. Yes, we are.

SHAMRAYEV. Hm . . . Well, splendid, splendid, but what are you going *in*, dear lady? We're carting the rye today – all the men are busy. And which horses were you thinking of using, may I ask?

ARKADINA. Which horses? How should *I* know?

SORIN. We've got carriage horses, haven't we?

SHAMRAYEV (*becoming agitated*). The carriage horses? But where am I going to get harness for them? Where am I going to get harness? Amazing, isn't it? Past comprehension! Dear lady! I revere your talent, I'll gladly give you ten years of my life, but horses I cannot give you!

ARKADINA. But supposing I *have* to go? What an extraordinary state of affairs!

SHAMRAYEV. Dear lady! You don't realise what farming involves!

ARKADINA (*flares up*). Oh, the same old story! In that case, I'm leaving for Moscow today. Have horses rented for me in the village – otherwise I shall *walk* to the station!

SHAMRAYEV (*flares up*). In that case I resign! Find yourself another steward!

Exit SHAMRAYEV.

ARKADINA. Every summer here it's the same, every summer I'm insulted! I'm not going to set foot in this place again!

Exit ARKADINA *left, where the bathing-place is assumed to be. A minute later she can be seen crossing towards the house, followed by* TRIGORIN *with his fishing-rods and bucket.*

SORIN (*flares up*). This is downright impertinence! This is downright heaven knows what! I'm sick of it, when all's said and done. Fetch all the horses directly!

NINA (*to* POLINA). But saying no to someone like that, a famous actress! Surely her slightest wish – her slightest whim, even – is more important than your farming? It's simply unbelievable!

POLINA (*in despair*). What can I do? Put yourself in my position. What can I do?

SORIN (*to* NINA). Come on, we'll go to my sister. We'll all plead with her not to leave. Isn't that right? (*Looks in the direction that* SHAMRAYEV *went off.*) The intolerable man! The tyrant!

NINA (*stops him getting up*). Sit down, sit down . . . We'll push you there . . .

She and MEDVEDENKO *push the wheelchair.*

How terrible, though!

SORIN. Yes, yes, it *is* terrible . . . But he won't go – I'll have a talk with him by and by.

They go off. Only DORN *and* POLINA *remain.*

DORN. How boring people are. Really your husband ought to

be thrown out on his neck, but in fact the whole thing will end with that old woman and his sister apologising to him. You'll see!

POLINA. He's sent the carriage horses out to the fields with all the others. Every day we have this sort of trouble. If you knew how it upsets me! It's making me ill – look, I'm shaking . . . He's so coarse – I can't bear it. (*Pleading.*) Yevgeni, my dear, my precious, take me unto you . . . Time's running out for us, we're not young any more, and oh, to stop hiding, even at the end of our lives, to stop lying . . .

Pause.

DORN. I'm fifty-five. It's a little late in the day to change my way of life.

POLINA. I know why you reject me – I know there are other women besides me. You can't take them all unto you. I understand that. Forgive me, I'm being tiresome.

NINA *appears near the house, picking flowers.*

DORN. No, no.

POLINA. I'm tormented by jealousy. Of course – you're a doctor – you can't avoid women. I understand that . . .

NINA *approaches.*

DORN. What's going on in there?

NINA. She's crying, and her brother's got his asthma.

DORN (*gets up*). I'd better go and give them both some drops . . .

NINA (*gives him the flowers*). Here, have these!

DORN. *Merci bien.* (*Goes towards the house.*)

POLINA (*going to him*). What lovely flowers! (*Near the house, in muffled tones.*) Give me those flowers! Give me those flowers!

As soon as she gets the flowers she tears them up and throws them on the ground. They both go into the house.

NINA (*alone*). How curious to see a famous actress crying, especially over such a tiny thing! And isn't this curious, too? – a famous writer, the darling of the public, someone they write about in all the papers, someone they sell pictures of, someone who's translated into foreign languages – and he spends the whole day fishing – he's delighted to have caught a couple of chub. I thought famous people were proud and unapproachable. I thought they despised the common herd – I thought their renown, the brilliance of their name, gave them a kind of revenge for the way the herd set birth and wealth above all else. But here they are crying, fishing, playing cards, laughing, and losing their tempers like everybody else . . .

Enter KONSTANTIN, *hatless, with a gun and a seagull he has killed.*

KONSTANTIN. You're alone?

NINA. Yes, I'm alone.

KONSTANTIN *lays the seagull at her feet.*

What does that signify?

KONSTANTIN. I had the dishonour to kill this seagull today. I'm laying it at your feet.

NINA. What's the matter with you? (*Picks the seagull up and looks at it.*)

KONSTANTIN (*after a pause*). Soon I shall kill myself in the same way.

NINA. You're not the person I used to know.

KONSTANTIN. No, I'm not. Not since you stopped being the person I used to know. You've changed towards me. You look at me coldly, you're embarrassed by my being here.

NINA. You've got so irritable recently. You put things obliquely all the time, in some kind of symbols. This seagull, too – this is obviously a symbol of something, but I'm sorry, I don't know what it means . . . (*Lays the seagull on the bench.*) I'm too simple to understand you.

KONSTANTIN. It all started that evening when my play was such an idiotic failure. Women never forgive failure. I burnt it, every last torn-up shred of it. If you knew how unhappy I am! It's terrifying the way you've grown cold towards me – it's unbelievable – it's as if I'd woken up and found that this lake had dried up, or drained away into the earth. You just said that you were too simple to understand me. Oh, what is there to understand? The play wasn't liked, you despise my inspiration, you've begun to think of me as an ordinary person – a nonentity – someone like everybody else . . . (*Stamps his foot.*) I know just what you mean, just exactly what you mean! It's like having a nail in my brain, curse it – and curse this pride of mine, too, that sucks my blood, sucks it like a serpent . . .

Sees TRIGORIN, *who is reading a book as he walks.*

Here comes the man with the real talent, entering like Hamlet, even down to the book. (*Mimics him.*) 'Words, words, words . . .' The sun hasn't reached you yet, and already you're smiling, your expression has melted in its rays. I won't stand in your way.

He quickly goes off.

TRIGORIN (*noting something down in the book*). Takes snuff and drinks vodka . . . Always in black. Loved by teacher . . .

NINA. Hello.

TRIGORIN. Hello to you. An unexpected turn of events, I gather, means that we are leaving today. It's hardly probable that you and I will see each other again. A pity. I don't often get the chance to meet girls of your age, not ones who are also interesting and attractive, and I can't remember now – can't clearly picture to myself – what it feels like to be eighteen or nineteen. So the girls who appear in my stories usually strike a false note. I should have liked to put myself in your place

for a while, just for an hour or so, to find out how your mind
worked and what sort of creature you were.

NINA. I should have liked to put myself in your place for a
while.

TRIGORIN. Why?

NINA. To know what it felt like to be a famous and talented
writer. What does fame feel like? What is the sensation of
being famous?

TRIGORIN. What does it feel like? It doesn't feel like anything,
so far as I know. I've never thought about it. (*After a moment's
reflection.*) Either you have an exaggerated idea of how famous
I am, or else it has no sensation at all.

NINA. But when you read about yourself in the papers?

TRIGORIN. If they're praising me it's nice. If they're abusing
me then I feel put out for a couple of days.

NINA. Strange and marvellous world! If you knew how I envied
you! People have such different lots in life. Some of them can
scarcely drag out their dull, obscure existence – all of them
alike, all of them unhappy; while others – you, for example
– you're one in a million – you're granted an absorbing, sunlit
life that's full of meaning . . . You're happy . . .

TRIGORIN. Me? (*Shrugs.*) Hm . . . You talk about fame and
happiness and some kind of absorbing, sunlit life, but to me
– forgive me – all these fine words are like those soft, sticky
sweets – the sort I never eat. You're very young and you're
very kind.

NINA. You have a wonderful life!

TRIGORIN. What's so specially good about it, though? (*Looks
at his watch.*) I have to go and write. I'm sorry, I'm rather
pressed for time . . . (*Laughs.*) You've trodden on my pet
corn, as they say, and I'm starting to get worked up and
slightly irritated. All right, then – let's talk about it. Let's talk
about my wonderful sunlit life . . . Now, where shall we
begin? (*After a moment's thought.*) There are things in this
world called *idées fixes*, when day and night a man can think

of nothing else except the moon, let's say. I have such a moon of my own. Day and night I am in the grip of a single obsession: I have to write, I have to write, I have to write . . . Scarcely have I finished one story than for some reason I have to write another, and then a third, and after the third a fourth . . . I write without cease, like a traveller with a fresh relay of horses waiting at every post, and I can't do otherwise. I ask you – what's sunlit or wonderful about that? It's a cruel life! Here I am talking to you, getting myself quite worked up, but at the same time I don't forget for a single moment that I have an unfinished story waiting for me. I see that cloud up there, looking like a grand piano, and I think, I shall have to put in a story somewhere that there was a cloud in the sky looking like a grand piano. I smell the scent of the heliotropes. I make a rapid mental note: cloying perfume, widow's purple, put in when describing summer evening. I catch us both up at every phrase, at every word, and I hasten to lock all these words and phrases away in my literary larder – you never know, they may come in handy! When I finish work I rush off to the theatre, or I go fishing; there at least I might relax and forget myself – but no, because inside my head a heavy iron ball is already beginning to shift – a new idea, and already I can feel the pull of my desk, and I have to rush off to write, write, write again. And that's how it always is, always and always, and I have no peace from myself, and I feel that I'm eating up my own life – that to make the honey I give to some remote reader I'm gathering the sweetness from my own best flowers – that I'm picking the flowers themselves and trampling their roots. I surely must be mad! My friends and relations surely can't be treating me like a sane man! 'What are you writing? What are you going to give us next?' Always the same thing, over and over again, and I get the feeling that this constant attention from my friends, this praise, this admiration, is all nothing but a trick, that I'm being lied to like an invalid, and sometimes I'm afraid they're just about to creep up on me from behind, that they're going to seize me like the wretched clerk in that story of Gogol's and cart me off to the madhouse. And in the years when I was a beginner still, the years when I was young, the best years, my trade was one long torment to me. The young writer – particularly when he's not successful – feels clumsy, inept, and useless; his nerves are on edge; he can't stop himself hanging round people connected with literature and art; an unacknowledged and unnoticed figure who's afraid to look people in the eye, like a compulsive gambler with no money. I couldn't see my reader, but in my imagination, for some reason, he was always someone unfriendly and mistrustful. I was afraid of the public, I found it terrifying, and whenever I had a new play produced I saw everyone with dark hair as antagonistic, and everyone with fair hair as coldly indifferent. It was terrible! It was a torment!

NINA. But surely inspiration, and the actual process of creation, give you moments of elevation, moments of happiness?

TRIGORIN. Yes, they do. When I'm writing it's rather agreeable. And reading the proofs – that's agreeable. But . . . scarcely has something come off the press than I can't bear it – I can see it's all wrong, it's a mistake, it should never have been written at all – and I feel disappointed, I feel deeply worthless . . . (*Laughs.*) But the public reads it and says: 'Yes, it's charming, it's clever . . . Charming, but nowhere near Tolstoy.' Or: 'It's a fine piece of writing, but Turgenev's *Fathers and Children* is better.' To my dying day it will go on being merely charming and clever, charming and clever, and nothing more, and when I'm dead my friends will say as they pass my grave: 'There lies Trigorin. He was a good writer, but he wasn't as good as Turgenev.'

NINA. Forgive me, but I refuse to understand what you're saying. You've simply been spoiled by success.

TRIGORIN. What success? I've never given any pleasure to myself. I don't like myself as a writer. The worst thing is that

I go round in some kind of daze, and often I don't understand what it is I'm writing . . . I love this water here, the trees, the sky; I have a feeling for nature – it arouses this passion I have, the irresistible desire to write. But then of course I'm not just a landscape-painter; I'm a citizen as well – I love my country, I love the common people. I feel that if I'm a writer then I have some obligation to deal with the people, with their sufferings and their future, to deal with science and the rights of man and so on and so forth; and deal with it all I do, in haste, urged on and snapped at on all sides. I rush back and forth like a fox bayed by hounds. I can see that life and science are getting further and further ahead of me all the time, while I fall further and further behind, like a peasant missing a train. And in the end I feel that all I can write is landscapes, and that in everything else I'm false – false to the marrow of my bones.

NINA. You've been overworking, and you haven't the time or the taste to become aware of your own importance. You may be dissatisfied with yourself, but in other people's eyes you're a great and wonderful man! If I were a writer like you I should sacrifice my whole life to the crowd – but I should know all the time that their happiness lay purely in reaching up to me, and they'd drag my chariot in triumph through the streets.

TRIGORIN. Dragging people in chariots, well . . . Agamemnon now, am I?

They both smile.

NINA. For the happiness of being a writer or an actress I'd put up with hunger and disappointment, and my family turning their backs on me. I'd live in a garret and eat black bread, I'd endure my dissatisfaction with myself and my consciousness of my own shortcomings; but then to make up for it I should demand glory . . . real resounding glory . . . (*Covers her face with her hands.*) My head's spinning . . . Oh . . . !

ARKADINA (*calls, off, from the house*). Boris! Boris?

TRIGORIN. I'm being summoned . . . Time to pack, I suppose. I don't feel like leaving, though. (*Looks around at the lake.*) Just look at the bounteousness of it . . . ! How fine!

NINA. You see the house and garden on the other side?

TRIGORIN. Yes.

NINA. My mother's dead now, but that was her estate. I was born there. I've spent my whole life around this lake – I know every little island in it.

TRIGORIN. A fine place you live in! (*Sees the seagull.*) What's that?

NINA. A seagull. Konstantin shot it.

TRIGORIN. Beautiful bird. I really don't feel like leaving. Why don't you try to persuade her to stay? (*Makes a note in his book.*)

NINA. What's that you're writing?

TRIGORIN. Nothing. Just jotting something down . . . An idea came into my head . . . (*Hides the book.*) An idea for a short story. A girl like you, living beside a lake since she was a child. She loves the lake the way a seagull might – she's as happy and free as a seagull. But one day by chance a man comes along and sees her. And quite idly he destroys her, like this seagull.

   Pause.
   ARKADINA *appears at the window.*

ARKADINA. Boris! Where are you?

TRIGORIN. Coming! (*Crosses to her, turning round to look at* NINA. *At the window, to* ARKADINA.) What is it?

ARKADINA. We're staying.

   Exit ARKADINA *into the house.*

NINA (*comes downstage and reflects for a moment*). A dream!

CURTAIN

Act Three

The dining-room in SORIN's *house. Doors left and right. Sideboard. Medicine cabinet. Dining-table in the middle of the room. Suitcase and cardboard boxes; signs of preparations for departure.* TRIGORIN *is eating lunch.* MASHA *is standing at the table.*

MASHA. I'm telling you all this because you're a writer. You can use it in something. Quite seriously, if he had wounded himself badly I couldn't have gone on living for another moment. I've got courage, though. I thought, 'Right!' – and I made up my mind to tear this love out of my heart, to tear it out by the roots.

TRIGORIN. How?

MASHA. I'm going to get married. To Medvedenko.

TRIGORIN. The schoolteacher?

MASHA. Yes.

TRIGORIN. I don't see the need for that.

MASHA. Loving without hope, waiting year after year for something to happen . . . I'm certainly not marrying for love, but I'll have new troubles to drown out the old. Be a change, anyway. Have another one, shall we?

TRIGORIN. Won't that be rather a lot?

MASHA. Oh, come on! (*Pours a glass each.*) There's no need to look at me like that. Women are more often drinkers than you realise. A few of them drink openly, like me, but most of them do it in secret. Oh yes. And always vodka or brandy. (*Clinks glasses.*) Here's to you! There's no nonsense about you – I'll be sorry to see you go.

They drink.

TRIGORIN. I don't much want to go myself.

MASHA. Ask her to stay, then.

TRIGORIN. No, she won't stay now. Her son's being extremely awkward. First he was trying to shoot himself; now, so I gather, he's going to challenge me to a duel. I don't know what for. He huffs and puffs, he preaches his 'new forms' . . . But there's room for all, surely, new and old alike – there's no need to elbow each other aside.

MASHA. How about jealousy? Not that it's any business of mine.

> *Pause.* YAKOV *crosses left to right with a suitcase.* NINA *enters and stops by the window.*

My schoolteacher isn't very clever, but he's a kind man, and he's poor, and he's very much in love with me. I feel sorry for him. I even feel sorry for his old mother. Anyway, let me wish you all the best. Remember me kindly. (*Shakes his hand warmly.*) I'm very grateful to you for taking an interest. Send me your books, though – and you must sign them! Don't put what you put for everybody else. Put 'To Masha, of dubious descent, and resident in this world for reasons unknown.' Goodbye!

> *Exit* MASHA.

NINA (*holding out a hand closed into a fist towards* TRIGORIN). Odds or evens?

TRIGORIN. Evens.

NINA (*sighs*). No. I've only got one bean in my hand. The question was, 'Should I become an actress or not?' If only someone could tell me!

TRIGORIN. It's not something that anyone *can* tell you.

NINA. We're saying goodbye to each other and . . . we may never see each other again. I should like to give you this little medallion to remember me by. I've had your initials engraved on it . . . and on this side the title of your book, *Days and Nights.*

TRIGORIN. What a very gracious gesture! (*Kisses the medallion.*)

It's a delightful present!

NINA. Remember me sometimes.

TRIGORIN. I shall remember you. I shall remember you as you were on that bright and sunny day – do you recall? – a week ago, when you were wearing a summer dress . . . and we had a talk . . . and there on the garden seat lay a white seagull.

NINA (*reflectively*). The seagull, yes . . . (*Pause.*) We can't say anything else – there are people coming . . . Give me two minutes before you leave, I beg of you.

> *She goes off left. As she does so* ARKADINA *enters right with* SORIN, *who is wearing a tailcoat with a decoration pinned to it, then* YAKOV, *who is preoccupied with collecting things up for the departure.*

ARKADINA. Now, why don't you stay at home, you poor old man? What do you want to go traipsing round calling on people for, with your rheumatism? (*To* TRIGORIN.) Who was that went out just now? Was that Nina?

TRIGORIN. Yes.

ARKADINA. *Pardon*, we're intruding . . . (*Sits.*) I think I've packed everything. What a torment it is.

TRIGORIN (*reads from the medallion*). *Days and Nights*, page 121, lines 11 and 12.

YAKOV (*clearing things from the table*). Am I to pack the fishing-rods, too?

TRIGORIN. Yes, I shall need them again. The books you can give away, though.

YAKOV. Sir.

TRIGORIN (*to himself*). Page 121, lines 11 and 12. What do they say? (*To* ARKADINA.) Have you got my books in the house?

ARKADINA. My brother's study – the corner cupboard.

TRIGORIN. Page 121 . . .

> *Exit* TRIGORIN.

ARKADINA. Really, Petrusha, I should stay at home if I

were you . . . .

SORIN. You're leaving. I shall get depressed sitting at home without you.

ARKADINA. What's happening in town, then?

SORIN. Nothing much, but all the same. (*Laughs.*) They're laying the foundation-stone for the new government building, etcetera, etcetera . . . I'd like to get out and about for an hour or two, anyway – I've been lying here like an old boot, stuck here like a gudgeon in the mud. I've ordered the horses for one o'clock, we can go together.

ARKADINA (*after a pause*). Well, you go on living here, then – don't get too bored, don't catch any colds. Keep an eye on my son. Look after him. Admonish him. (*Pause.*) I'm leaving, so I'll never know why Konstantin tried to shoot himself. The main reason, I think, was jealousy, and the sooner I take Trigorin away from here the better.

SORIN. I don't know quite how to put this, but there were other reasons, too. There he is, no question about it – young man, intelligent, he lives in the country, miles from anywhere, and he's no money, no position, no future. Nothing to do. He's ashamed of his idleness – he's frightened of it. I'm devoted to him and he's quite attached to me, but when all's said and done he feels there's no place for him in the house – he feels like a poor relation here, a parasite. Pride, no question about it . . .

ARKADINA. Oh, he's a trial to me! (*Lost in thought.*) Maybe he should get a job . . .

SORIN (*whistles for a moment, then, irresolutely*). I wonder if the best thing wouldn't be for you to . . . give him a little money. The first thing he needs to do is to dress like a normal human being, it's as simple as that. Look, he's been wearing that one same jacket for the past three years. He hasn't got an overcoat to his back . . . . (*Laughs.*) Then again it wouldn't hurt the boy to see a bit of the world . . . Go abroad, perhaps . . . It really wouldn't cost all that much.

ARKADINA. All the same . . . I suppose I might arrange a little more for clothes, but as for going abroad . . . No, at the moment I can't even manage the clothes. (*Decisively.*) I've no money!

SORIN *laughs.*

I haven't!

SORIN (*whistles for a moment*). Well, there we are. Forgive me. Don't be angry, my dear. I believe you . . . You're a good and generous woman.

ARKADINA (*on the verge of tears*). I've no money!

SORIN. If I had any money, no question, I'd give him some myself, but I've nothing, not a kopeck. (*Laughs.*) My entire pension is taken by that steward of mine to spend on planting crops and raising cattle and keeping bees, and I might as well pour it straight down the drain. The bees drop dead, the cows drop dead, and they never let me have any horses . . .

ARKADINA. All right, I have money, but I happen to be in the theatrical profession – my outfits alone have nearly ruined me.

SORIN. You're a dear kind girl . . . I respect your feelings . . . Yes . . . But I think I'm having another of my . . . you know . . . (*Staggers.*) Head's going round. (*Holds on to the table.*) Not feeling too good, simple as that.

ARKADINA (*frightened*). Petrusha! (*Trying to support him.*) Petrusha, my dear . . . (*Calls.*) Help me! Help . . . !

Enter KONSTANTIN, *his head bandaged, and*
MEDVEDENKO.

ARKADINA. He's ill!

SORIN. I'm all right, I'm all right . . . (*Smiles and drinks some water.*) It's passed off . . . simple as that . . .

KONSTANTIN (*to his mother*). There's no need to be frightened, Mama, it's not dangerous. Uncle often has these turns now. Uncle, you must have a lie-down.

SORIN. For a moment, yes . . . I'm still going into town. I'll have a little lie-down, then I'll go . . . no question about it . . .

He begins to go off, leaning on his stick.

MEDVEDENKO (*taking his arm*). There's a riddle: in the morning on four, at midday on two, in the evening on three . . .

SORIN (*laughs*). Quite. And at night on your back. Thank you – I can manage on my own . . .

MEDVEDENKO. Well, there's politeness . . .

Exeunt MEDVEDENKO and SORIN.

ARKADINA. He gave me such a fright!

KONSTANTIN. It's bad for his health, living in the country. He's pining away. Now, Mama, if you had a sudden attack of generosity and lent him a couple of thousand rubles he could live in town all year.

ARKADINA. I haven't any money. I'm an actress, not a bank-manager.

Pause.

KONSTANTIN. Will you change my dressing, Mama. You do it so nicely.

ARKADINA (*gets iodoform and dressings out of the medicine cabinet*). The doctor's late, though.

KONSTANTIN. He promised to be here at ten, and it's twelve already.

ARKADINA. Sit down. (*Takes the bandage off his head.*) You look as if you're wearing a turban. Someone who came to the kitchen door yesterday was asking what nationality you were. It's nearly healed, though. Only the merest trifle left to go. (*Kisses him on the head.*) You're not going to start playing with guns again while I'm away, are you.

KONSTANTIN. No, Mama. That was just a moment of crazy

despair when I lost control of myself. It won't happen again. (*Kisses her hand.*) You have magic in your hands. I remember a long time ago, when you were still working in the State theatre – when I was little – there was a fight in the courtyard of our block, and a washerwoman living in one of the apartments got badly knocked about. Do you remember? When they picked her up she was unconscious . . . You kept going to see her, you took her medicine, you bathed the children in her washtub. Surely you remember?

ARKADINA. No. (*Puts a new bandage on.*)

KONSTANTIN. There were two ballet-dancers living in the same block . . . They used to come and have coffee with you . . .

ARKADINA. I remember that.

KONSTANTIN. They were terribly religious. (*Pause.*) These last few days I've loved you as tenderly and whole-heartedly as I did when I was a child. I've no one left apart from you. But why, why has that man come between us?

ARKADINA. Konstantin, you don't understand him. He's someone of the highest integrity . . .

KONSTANTIN. However, when they told him I was going to challenge him to a duel his integrity didn't hinder his cowardice. He's leaving. Ignominiously fleeing!

ARKADINA. Oh, nonsense! I'm taking him away. You can't be pleased by our relationship, of course, but you're perfectly intelligent, and I must insist that you respect my freedom.

KONSTANTIN. I do respect your freedom, but you must allow me to be free, too, you must let me have my own opinion of that man. Someone of the highest integrity! Here we are on the point of quarrelling over him while he sits in the drawing-room or the garden somewhere laughing at us . . . Educating Nina, trying to convince her once and for all that he's a genius.

ARKADINA. You take pleasure in being disagreeable to me. That man is someone I have great respect for, and I must ask you not to speak ill of him in my presence.

KONSTANTIN. I don't have great respect for him, however. You want me to think he's a genius as well, but I'm sorry, I can't tell a lie – his work nauseates me.

ARKADINA. That's jealousy. People with no talent themselves, only pretensions, are always reduced to running down people who do have real talent. It must be a great comfort!

KONSTANTIN (*ironically*). Real talent! (*Furiously.*) I've more talent than the lot of you, if it comes to that! (*Tears the bandage off his head.*) You and your dull, plodding friends have got a stranglehold on art, and the only things you consider legitimate and real are the ones you do yourselves – everything else you crush and smother! I don't acknowledge any of you! I don't acknowledge you, I don't acknowledge him!

ARKADINA. And what are you? A Decadent!

KONSTANTIN. Go off to your nice little theatre and act in your miserable mediocre plays!

ARKADINA. I've never acted in plays like that in my life! Leave me alone! You couldn't write so much as a miserable farce! You shopkeeper! Yes – Kiev shopkeeper! Parasite!

KONSTANTIN. Miser!

ARKADINA. Ragbag!

KONSTANTIN *sits down and weeps quietly.*

Nonentity! (*Passing to agitation.*) Don't cry. There's no need to cry . . . (*Weeps.*) You mustn't cry . . . (*Kisses him on his brow, his cheeks, his head.*) My own dear child, forgive me . . . Forgive your wicked mother. Forgive your unhappy mother.

KONSTANTIN (*embraces her*). If only you knew! I've lost everything. She doesn't love me, I can't write any more . . . All my hopes have foundered . . .

ARKADINA. Don't despair . . . Everything will be all right. I'm taking him away now – she'll go back to loving you. (*Wipes his tears.*) Enough, enough. We're friends again.

KONSTANTIN (*kisses her hands*). Yes, Mama.

ARKADINA (*gently*). Be friends with him, too. No duels . . . You won't, will you?

KONSTANTIN. Very well . . . But please, Mama, I don't want to meet him. It's hard for me . . . more than I can bear . . .

Enter TRIGORIN.

So . . . I'm going . . . (*Quickly puts the medical supplies back in the cabinet.*) The doctor can do the dressing later . . .

TRIGORIN (*searches in a book*). Page 121 . . . Lines 11 and 12 . . . Here we are . . . (*Reads.*) 'If ever you have need of my life, then come and take it.'

KONSTANTIN *picks up the bandage from the floor and goes out.*

ARKADINA (*glancing at the clock*). They'll be bringing the horses very shortly.

TRIGORIN (*to himself*). If ever you have need of my life, then come and take it.

ARKADINA. You're packed, I hope?

TRIGORIN (*impatiently*). Yes, yes . . . (*Lost in thought.*) Why do I hear a note of sadness in that cry from a pure heart, and why has my own heart so painfully contracted . . . ? If ever you have need of my life, then come and take it. (*To* ARKADINA.) Let's stop another day!

ARKADINA *shakes her head.*

Just one more day!

ARKADINA. My dear, I know what keeps you here. But do take a hold of yourself. You're a little intoxicated – you must be sober again.

TRIGORIN. You must be sober, too – be understanding and sensible, I implore you – see all this like the true friend you are . . . (*Presses her hand.*) You're capable of sacrifice . . . Be my friend – let me go . . .

ARKADINA (*in great agitation*). You're as captivated as that?

TRIGORIN. I feel as if a voice were calling me to her! Perhaps this is the very thing I need.

ARKADINA. Some provincial girl's love? How little you understand yourself!

TRIGORIN. Sometimes people fall asleep on their feet – and that's how I am now, talking to you but feeling all the time as if I were asleep and dreaming of her . . . Sweet and marvellous dreams have taken hold of me . . . Let me go . . .

ARKADINA (*trembling*). No, no . . . I'm a woman like any other – you can't speak to me so . . . Don't torment me, Boris . . . It frightens me . . .

TRIGORIN. If you choose you can be a woman unlike any other. A young love – a love full of charm and poetry – bearing me off into the land of dreams . . . in all this wide world no one but her can give me happiness! The sort of love I've never known yet . . . I'd no time for it when I was young, when I was beating on editors' doors, when I was struggling with poverty . . . Now here it is, that love I never knew – it's come, it's calling to me . . . What sense in running away from it?

ARKADINA (*with fury*). You've gone mad!

TRIGORIN. Release me, then.

ARKADINA. You've all conspired to torment me today! (*Weeps.*)

TRIGORIN (*clutches his head*). She doesn't understand! She won't understand!

ARKADINA. Am I really so old and ugly that you can talk to me about other women without so much as batting an eyelid? (*Embraces and kisses him.*) Oh, you're out of your senses! My wonderful man, my marvellous man . . . The last page of my life! (*Kneels.*) My joy, my pride, my delight . . . (*Embraces his knees.*) Leave me for a single hour and I'll never survive it, I'll go mad, my amazing man, my magnificent man, my sovereign lord . . .

TRIGORIN. Someone may come in. (*Helps her to her feet.*)

ARKADINA. Let them – I'm not ashamed of my love for you. (*Kisses his hands.*) My treasure, my wild and desperate man, you want to behave like a lunatic, but I don't want you to, I won't let you . . . (*Laughs.*) You're mine . . . you're mine . . . This brow of yours is mine, these eyes are mine, this lovely silken hair is mine . . . You're all mine. You're such a talented man, such an intelligent man, you're the finest writer alive today, you're the sole hope of Russia . . . You have so much sincerity, so much simplicity and freshness and wholesome humour . . . With one stroke you're able to convey the essence of a person or a landscape, your characters live and breathe. Impossible to read you without delight! You think this is mere incense at your altar? That I'm flattering you? Look into my eyes . . . look into them . . . Do I look like a liar? See for yourself – I'm the only one who can appreciate you, the only one who tells you the truth, my sweet, my marvel . . . You'll come away? Yes? You won't abandon me . . .?

TRIGORIN. I've no will of my own . . . I've never had a will of my own . . . Flabby, crumbling, endlessly submissive – is that really what pleases a woman? Pick me up, carry me off – just don't let me out of your sight for an instant.

ARKADINA (*to herself*). Now he's mine. (*Easily, as if nothing had happened*). Anyway, you can stay if you like. I'll go, and you can come on later, in a week's time. There's really no reason for you to hurry, is there?

TRIGORIN. No, no, we'll go together.

ARKADINA. Whichever you like. Together – all right, together . . .

Pause. TRIGORIN *notes something down in his book.*

What's that?

TRIGORIN. I heard a rather nice turn of phrase this morning – 'Virgins' forest . . .' Might come in handy. (*Stretches.*) So, we're going to be travelling? Stations and carriages again, station restaurants and station cutlets, conversations on trains . . .

Enter SHAMRAYEV.

SHAMRAYEV. I have to inform you, with the utmost regret, that the horses are ready. It's time, dear lady, to go to the station; the train arrives at five minutes after two. Now you won't forget, if you will be so kind, to inquire into the whereabouts of that actor, Suzdaltzev? Is he alive and well? We used to go drinking together once upon a time . . . His performance in *The Great Mail Robbery* was beyond compare . . . At that time, as I recall, he was working with the tragedian Izmailov – another remarkable character . . . Don't hurry yourself, dear lady, another five minutes yet. Once, in some melodrama, they were playing conspirators, and when they were suddenly discovered he was supposed to say: 'Caught, like rats in a trap!' Izmailov – 'Caught, like trats in a rap!' (*Laughs.*) Trats in a rap!

While he has been speaking, YAKOV *has been busy with the suitcases, the* MAID *has been bringing* ARKADINA *her hat, coat, umbrella, and gloves, and everyone has been helping her to put her things on. The* MAN COOK *has looked in from the lefthand door, and then a few moments later come uncertainly all the way in. Enter* POLINA, *followed later by* SORIN *and* MEDVEDENKO.

POLINA (*offering a punnet*). Some plums for the journey . . . They're very sweet. You might feel like something nice . . .

ARKADINA. That's very kind of you.

POLINA. Goodbye, my dear. If anything was not as it should have been then please forgive me. (*Weeps.*)

ARKADINA (*embraces her*). Everything was fine, everything was fine. Only you mustn't start crying.

POLINA. Our lives are running out!

ARKADINA. But what can we do?

> SORIN, *wearing hat and Inverness, and carrying a stick, comes out of the lefthand door and crosses the room.*

SORIN. Time to go. You don't want to be late, when all's said and done. I'm going to get in.

> *Exit* SORIN.

MEDVEDENKO. Yes, and I'm going to walk to the station . . . See you off. I'll have to look sharp . . .

> *Exit* MEDVEDENKO.

ARKADINA. Goodbye, then, my dears . . . We'll see each other again next summer, if we're spared . . .

> *The* MAID, YAKOV, *and the* COOK *kiss her hand.*

Don't forget me.

> *Gives the* COOK *a ruble.*

Here, a ruble. That's for all three of you.

COOK. Thank you kindly, ma'am. Have a good journey, now! Very grateful to you!

YAKOV. God send you good fortune!

SHAMRAYEV. Give us the pleasure of hearing from you! (*To* TRIGORIN.) Goodbye, then.

ARKADINA. Where's Konstantin? Will you tell him I'm going? I must say goodbye to him. Well, then, remember me kindly. (*To* YAKOV.) I gave cook a ruble. That's for all three of you.

> *They all go off right. The stage is empty. Noises off, of the sort that occur when people are being said goodbye to. The* MAID *comes back and takes the basket of plums off the table, then goes out again.* TRIGORIN *comes back in.*

TRIGORIN. I've forgotten my stick. I think it's out on the verandah.

Crosses towards the lefthand door and meets NINA *as she enters.*

There you are. We're leaving.

NINA. I had a feeling we'd see each other again. (*Excitedly.*) I've made up my mind, once and for all – I'm going on the stage. By tomorrow I shan't be here – I'm getting away from my father, I'm abandoning everything, I'm starting a new life . . . I'm leaving, just like you . . . for Moscow. We shall see each other there.

TRIGORIN (*looking round*). Stay at the Slavyansky Bazar . . . Let me know as soon as you arrive . . . Grokholsky's house, on Molchanovka . . . I must hurry . . .

   Pause

NINA. Another minute . . .

TRIGORIN (*keeping his voice down*). You're so lovely . . . Oh, what joy it is to think we shall be seeing each other again before long!

   She lays her head against his chest.

I shall see those marvellous eyes again, this inexpressibly lovely, tender smile . . . these gentle features, this look of angelic innocence . . . My dear . . .

A prolonged kiss.   oh no she didn't

CURTAIN

Act Four

Two years have elapsed.

One of the reception-rooms in SORIN's *house which* KONSTANTIN *has turned into a working study. Doors left and right leading to inner rooms. A glass door, centre, opening on to the verandah. Apart from the usual living-room furniture there is a writing table in the righthand corner, a Turkish divan beside the lefthand door, a cupboard full of books, and more books on the window-ledges and chairs. – Evening. A single shaded lamp is alight. Twilight. The sighing of the trees can be heard, and the howling of the wind in the chimneys. The sound of the watchman's rattle as he passes. Enter* MEDVEDENKO *and* MASHA.

MASHA (*calls*). Hello? Are you there? (*Looks round.*) No one. The old man keeps asking every minute, 'Where's Kostya? Where's Konstantin?' He can't live without him . . .

MEDVEDENKO. He's frightened of being alone. (*Listens.*) What terrible weather! All yesterday, too, all last night.

MASHA (*turns up the lamp*). There are waves on the lake. Huge waves.

MEDVEDENKO. The garden's quite dark. They should tell someone to knock down that theatre. It's as hideous as bare bones, and the curtain slaps in the wind. When I was going past yesterday evening I could have sworn there was someone crying in there.

MASHA. Well, then . . .

Pause.

MEDVEDENKO. Let's go home, Masha!

MASHA (*shakes her head*). I'm staying the night.

MEDVEDENKO (*pleading*). Masha, let's go! The baby could be

hungry, who knows?

MASHA. Oh, fiddle. Matryona will feed him.

Pause.

MEDVEDENKO. It's a shame, though. This will be his third night without his mother.

MASHA. What a bore you've become. At least it was philosophical vapourings before – now it's the baby and let's go home all the time, the baby and let's go home – I never hear anything else out of you.

MEDVEDENKO. Let's go, Masha!

MASHA. You go.

MEDVEDENKO. Your father won't give me any horses.

MASHA. Yes, he will. Just ask him – he'll give you some.

MEDVEDENKO. Well, perhaps I'll ask him. So you'll be coming tomorrow?

MASHA (*takes a pinch of snuff*). Yes, yes, tomorrow. You keep badgering away . . .

> *Enter* KONSTANTIN *and* POLINA. KONSTANTIN *has brought pillows and a blanket, and* POLINA *bed-linen. They put all this on the Turkish divan, then* KONSTANTIN *crosses to his desk and sits down.*

What's that for, Mama?

POLINA. He's asked to have a bed made up for him in here with Konstantin.

MASHA. I'll do it . . . (*She makes up the bed.*)

POLINA (*sighs*). Second childhood . . . (*Crosses to the writing table, rests her elbows on it, and looks at a manuscript. Pause.*)

MEDVEDENKO. I'll be off, then. Goodbye, Masha. (*Kisses his wife's hand.*) Goodbye, Mother. (*Tries to kiss his mother-in-law's hand.*)

POLINA (*with annoyance*). Oh, come on, now! Off you go.

MEDVEDENKO (*to* KONSTANTIN). Goodbye, then.

KONSTANTIN *proffers his hand in silence. Exit*
MEDVEDENKO.

POLINA (*looking at the manuscript*). No one ever dreamed you'd
turn out to be a real writer, Kostya. But now, thanks be to
God, you've even started to get money from those literary
magazines. (*Runs her hand through his hair.*) You've turned
into a handsome man, too . . . Dear Kostya, be a good boy,
now, and be a bit kinder to my poor Masha . . .!

MASHA (*making the bed*). Leave him, Mama.

POLINA (*to* KONSTANTIN). She's a sweet, good girl. (*Pause.*)
All a woman needs, Kostya, is the odd kind glance. I know
from my own experience.

KONSTANTIN *gets up from his desk and silently leaves the
room.*

MASHA. Now you've put his back up. What did you have to go
badgering him for?

POLINA. I feel sorry for you, Masha.

MASHA. A lot of help that is.

POLINA. My heart aches for you. Do you think I can't see
what's happening? Do you think I don't understand?

MASHA. It's all nonsense. Love without hope – that's just in
novels. Fiddle! You mustn't lose your grip on yourself, that's
all, you mustn't keep waiting for something to happen, like
a sailor waiting for the weather . . . Once love has dug itself
into your heart you have to get it out again. They've promised
to transfer my husband to another district. As soon as we've
got there I shall forget it all . . . I shall tear it out of my heart
by the roots.

A melancholy waltz can be heard from the next room but one.

POLINA. That's Kostya playing. He's down in the dumps,
then.

MASHA (*noiselessly performs one or two turns of the waltz*). The main thing, Mama, is not to have him in front of my eyes all the time. Just let them give Semyon his transfer and, believe me, in a month I shall have forgotten him. So fiddle-de-dee.

The lefthand door opens. SORIN, *in his wheelchair, is pushed in by* DORN *and* MEDVEDENKO.

MEDVEDENKO. I've got six of us at home now. With flour at two kopecks a pound.

DORN. You'll just have to manage.

MEDVEDENKO. Yes, you can laugh. You've got plenty of money.

DORN. Money? In thirty years of practice, my friend, thirty years of unrelenting practice, when night and day I couldn't call my soul my own, I managed to save a miserable two thousand rubles – and even that I went through while I was abroad just now. I've nothing.

MASHA (*to her husband*). Haven't you gone?

MEDVEDENKO (*guiltily*). How can I? When they won't give me any horses!

MASHA (*with bitter irritation, lowering her voice*). I just want you out of my sight!

The wheelchair comes to a halt in the lefthand half of the room. POLINA, MASHA, *and* DORN *sit down beside it.* MEDVEDENKO *moves sadly aside.*

DORN. So many changes here, though! You've turned this drawing-room into a study.

MASHA. It's more convenient for Konstantin, working in here. He can go out into the garden to think whenever he feels like it.

The watchman's rattle, off.

SORIN. Where's my sister?

DORN. Gone to the station to meet Trigorin. Back in a moment.

SORIN. If you thought it necessary to get my sister here then

I must be dangerously ill. (*Falls silent for a moment.*) A fine business, I must say – here I am, dangerously ill, and they won't give me any medicine.

DORN. What would you like, then? Valerian drops? Bicarbonate of soda? Quinine?

SORIN. Yes, and now we get the moralising. Oh, what a penance it is! (*Nodding at the divan.*) Is that made up for me?

POLINA. For you, yes.

SORIN. Thank you.

> DORN *hums to himself.*

Now, I should like to give Kostya an idea for a story. It would be entitled: *The Man who wanted to.* Once, when I was young, I wanted to become a man of letters – and I never became one. I wanted to speak well – and I've always spoken appallingly. (*Mimics himself.*) 'Simple as that, etcetera etcetera . . . I mean . . . you know . . .' – I used to drag out a summing-up to such lengths I'd break into a sweat. I wanted to get married – and I never got married. I wanted always to live in town – and here I am ending my days in the country, simple as that.

DORN. You wanted to get to the fourth grade of the civil service – and you did.

SORIN (*laughs*). I wasn't trying for that. That came of its own accord.

DORN. Come now, giving vent to your dissatisfaction with life at the age of sixty-two is not very handsome.

SORIN. It's like talking to the gatepost. Can't you get it into your head that I want to live?

DORN. That's fatuous. According to the laws of nature every life must have an end.

SORIN. You speak as someone who's eaten his fill. You've had your fill so you're indifferent to life – it's all one to you. But even you will dread to die.

DORN. The dread of death is an animal dread . . . It has to be suppressed. The only people who can rationally fear death are the ones who believe in eternal life, and who dread for their sins. But firstly, you're an unbeliever, and secondly – what are your sins? You served twenty-five years in the Department of Justice, that's all!

SORIN (*laughs*). Twenty-eight...

> *Enter* KONSTANTIN. *He sits down on a stool at* SORIN's *feet.* MASHA *does not take her eyes off him all the time he is there.*

DORN. We're stopping Konstantin from working.

KONSTANTIN. No, it's all right.

> *Pause.*

MEDVEDENKO. May I ask you, Doctor, which foreign city you liked best?

DORN. Genoa.

KONSTANTIN. Why Genoa?

DORN. There's a splendid street life there. When you come out of your hotel in the evening the whole street is jammed with people. You wander aimlessly about in the crowd, hither and thither, this way that way, and you share its life, you spiritually merge with it. You begin to believe that it would in fact be possible to have a single world soul of the sort that your friend Nina once acted in your play. Where is she now, by the way? Where is she and how is she?

KONSTANTIN. She's well, as far as I know.

DORN. I heard she was leading some strange sort of life. What's it all about?

KONSTANTIN. It's a long story, Doctor.

DORN. In a nutshell.

> *Pause.*

KONSTANTIN. She ran away from home and took up with Trigorin. You know that much?

DORN. I know that much.

KONSTANTIN. She had a child. The child died. Trigorin decided he was no longer in love with her and reverted to his former attachment, as was only to be expected. Not that he'd ever given it up. Being the spineless creature that he is he'd somehow contrived to keep a foothold in both camps. So far as I can make out, Nina's private life has not been a total success.

DORN. How about the stage?

KONSTANTIN. Even worse, I think. She made her debut at a summer theatre outside Moscow, and then went to the provinces. I wasn't letting her out of my sight at that point, and for some time wherever she went I went, too. She kept taking on big parts, but she played them crudely and vulgarly, with a lot of howling and sawing of the air. There were moments when she showed some talent in shouting, or dying, but they were only moments.

DORN. So there is talent there, at any rate?

KONSTANTIN. It was difficult to tell. There probably is. I could see her, but she wouldn't see me, and her maid would never let me into her room. I undertood her feelings, and I didn't insist. (*Pause.*) What else can I tell you? When I was home again I started getting letters from her. Intelligent, warm, interesting letters. She never complained, but I could sense that she was deeply unhappy, that there was a sick nervous strain in every line. Even her imagination was a little distraught. She'd sign herself 'The Seagull'. It was like that play of Pushkin's where the old miller goes mad with grief and says he's a raven. She kept saying in the letters that she was a seagull. Now she's here.

DORN. How do you mean, here?

KONSTANTIN. In town, at the inn. She's been living in a room there for the best part of a week. I'd have gone to call on her – in fact Masha here did go – but she won't see anyone. Semyon says he saw her yesterday evening, in the fields a mile or so from here.

MEDVEDENKO. Yes, I did. She was going away from here, towards town. I said hello to her and asked why she didn't come to see us. She said she would.

KONSTANTIN. She won't, though. (*Pause.*) Her father and stepmother have disowned her. They've put watchmen everywhere to stop her even getting near the estate.

Crosses to his writing-table with the doctor.

How easy it is, Doctor, to be a philosopher on paper, and how difficult to be one in real life!

SORIN. She was a delightful girl.

DORN. I beg your pardon?

SORIN. I said she was a delightful girl. One former civil servant of the fourth grade was even in love with her for a while.

DORN. You old rake.

SHAMRAYEV laughs, off.

POLINA. It sounds as if they've arrived from the station.

KONSTANTIN. Yes, I can hear Mama.

Enter ARKADINA and TRIGORIN, followed by SHAMRAYEV.

SHAMRAYEV (*as he enters*). We're all getting older, we're all getting a little weather-beaten – but you, dear lady, go on being young . . . Dressed in light colours, full of life and grace . . .

ARKADINA. You're tempting fortune again, you tiresome man!

TRIGORIN (*to SORIN*). Hello! Still not better, then? We can't have that! (*Joyfully, at the sight of MASHA.*) And you're here!

MASHA. You recognised me, then? (*Shakes hands.*)

TRIGORIN. Married?

MASHA. Long since.

TRIGORIN. Happy?

He exchanges bows with DORN and MEDVEDENKO, then goes uncertainly up to KONSTANTIN.

I'm told you're ready to let bygones be bygones.

　　KONSTANTIN *holds out his hand.*

ARKADINA (*to her son*). He's brought the magazine with your new story.

KONSTANTIN (*to* TRIGORIN, *taking the volume*). Thank you. Most kind.

　　They sit.

TRIGORIN. I bring greetings from all your admirers. You're the talk of Petersburg and Moscow alike, and people keep asking me about you. They want to know what sort of person you are – how old – are you fair or are you dark? They all think you're middle-aged, I don't know why. And no one knows your real name, since you always publish under a pen-name. You're as mysterious as the Man in the Iron Mask.

KONSTANTIN. Are you here for long?

TRIGORIN. No, I'm leaving for Moscow tomorrow. I have to. I'm rushing to finish a story, and then I've promised something for a collection. Life as ever, in a word.

　　While they are talking, ARKADINA *and* POLINA *are setting up a card-table in the middle of the room and putting a cloth on it.* SHAMRAYEV *is lighting the candles and setting chairs. They get a lotto set out of the cupboard.*

Not a very warm welcome from the weather. A cruel wind. In the morning, if it drops, I'm going down to the lake for some fishing. I must take a look at the garden as I go, and the spot where your play was performed – do you remember? I've been developing an idea for a story. I just need to refresh my memory of the setting.

MASHA (*to her father*). Let my husband take a horse! He's got to get home.

SHAMRAYEV (*mimics her*). Horse . . . home . . . (*Sternly.*) You know as well as I do – they've just been out to the station.

They can't go running all over the countryside again.

MASHA. There *are* other horses . . . (*Sees that her father is not responding and flaps her hand.*) Oh, what's the use . . . ?

MEDVEDENKO. Masha, I'll walk. Really . . .

POLINA (*sighs*). Walk, in weather like this . . . (*Sits down at the card-table.*) Come on, then, everyone.

MEDVEDENKO. I mean, it's only three miles or so . . . Goodbye . . . (*Kisses his wife's hand.*) Goodbye, Mother. (*His mother-in-law reluctantly gives him her hand to be kissed.*) I wouldn't disturb anyone, only it's the baby . . . (*Bows to everyone.*) Goodbye . . .

Exit MEDVEDENKO, *with apologetic gait.*

SHAMRAYEV. I dare say he'll manage it. He's not a general.

POLINA (*raps on the table*). Come on, then. Let's not waste time – they'll be calling us for supper in a minute.

SHAMRAYEV, MASHA, and DORN sit down at the table.

ARKADINA (*to* TRIGORIN). When the long autumn evenings come they play lotto here. Look – an antique set that we used when our poor mother played with us as children. Won't you try a round with us before supper?

Sits down with TRIGORIN *at the table.*

It's a boring game, but it's all right when you get used to it.

She gives everyone three cards each.

KONSTANTIN (*leafing through the magazine*). He's read his own story, and he hasn't even cut the pages of mine.

He puts the magazine down on his writing-table, then goes to the lefthand door. As he passes his mother he kisses her head.

ARKADINA. How about you, Kostya?

KONSTANTIN. Will you excuse me? I don't really feel like it . . . I'm going to walk up and down for a bit.

Exit KONSTANTIN.

ARKADINA. The stake is ten kopecks. Put in for me, will you, Doctor.

DORN. Ma'am.

MASHA. Has everyone put in? I'm starting . . . Twenty-two!

ARKADINA. Yes.

MASHA. Three!

DORN. Right.

MASHA. Have you put it on? Eighty-one! Ten!

SHAMRAYEV. Not so fast.

ARKADINA. Oh, but my dears, the reception I got in Kharkov! My head is still spinning!

MASHA. Thirty-four!

A melancholy waltz is played, off.

ARKADINA. The students gave me an ovation . . . Three baskets of flowers, two garlands, and this . . . (*Takes a brooch off her breast and throws it on to the table.*)

SHAMRAYEV. Oh, yes! Yes, indeed!

MASHA. Fifty . . . !

DORN. Fifty-what? Just fifty?

ARKADINA. I was wearing an amazing outfit . . . Whatever else, I do know how to dress.

POLINA. That's Kostya playing. The poor boy's pining.

SHAMRAYEV. They're being very rude about him in the papers.

MASHA. Seventy-seven!

ARKADINA. Why does he pay any attention?

TRIGORIN. He's not having much success. He still just can't find his own voice. There's something odd and formless about his work – something verging at times on the nightmarish. Never a single living character.

MASHA. Eleven!

ARKADINA (*glances at* SORIN). Petrusha, is this boring for you?

(*Pause*.) He's asleep.

DORN. One former civil servant of the fourth grade is fast asleep.

MASHA. Seven! Ninety!

TRIGORIN. If I'd lived on an estate like this, beside a lake, do you think I should ever have taken up writing? I should have wrestled the passion down, and done nothing but fish.

MASHA. Twenty-eight!

TRIGORIN. To catch a ruff or a perch – that is perfect happiness!

DORN. I believe in the boy, though. There's something there! There's something there! He thinks in images, his stories are bright and colourful, and they speak to me strongly. The only sad thing is that he doesn't have any clear aims. He produces an impression but nothing more, and you can't get all that far on impressions alone. (*To* ARKADINA.) Are you pleased to have a son who's a writer?

ARKADINA. Can you imagine, I still haven't read anything by him. I never have time.

MASHA. Twenty-six!

KONSTANTIN *comes quietly in and goes to his desk.*

SHAMRAYEV (*to* TRIGORIN). And we still have one of your things here.

TRIGORIN. What's that?

SHAMRAYEV. Konstantin somehow managed to shoot a seagull, and you told me to have it stuffed.

TRIGORIN. I don't remember that. (*Reflecting.*) No recollection!

MASHA. Sixty-six! One!

KONSTANTIN (*flings open the window and listens*). Pitch dark. I can't think why I feel so uneasy.

ARKADINA. Kostya, shut the window, there's a draft.

KONSTANTIN *shuts the window.*

MASHA. Eighty-eight!

TRIGORIN. Ladies and gentlemen, I have a full house.

ARKADINA (*merrily*). Bravo! Bravo!

SHAMRAYEV. Bravo!

ARKADINA. Always, wherever he goes, that man has all the luck. (*Gets up.*) Now let's go and have something to eat, though. Our visiting celebrity hasn't had a proper meal today. We'll go on again after supper. (*To her son.*) Kostya, leave your writing – let's go and eat.

KONSTANTIN. I won't, Mama. I'm not hungry.

ARKADINA. As you wish.

Wakes SORIN.

Petrusha – supper!

Takes SHAMRAYEV's *arm.*

I'll tell you all about the reception I got in Kharkov . . .

POLINA *extinguishes the candles on the table, then she and* DORN *push the wheelchair. They all go out through the lefthand door.* KONSTANTIN *remains alone on stage at his writing table.*

KONSTANTIN (*about to write, runs through what he has written already*). I've talked so much about new forms, and now I feel I'm gradually slipping into the same old pattern myself. (*Reads*) 'The poster on the fence was announcing to the world . . . Her pale face, framed by her dark hair . . .' 'Announcing to the world . . .' 'framed . . .' It's undistinguished. (*Deletes.*) I'll start with the man being woken by the sound of the rain, and all the rest can go. The description of the moonlit night – that's long and laboured. Trigorin has developed his special little tricks – it's easy for him . . . He has the neck of a broken bottle glittering on the bank of the millpool and the shadow of the water-wheel black beside it – and there's his moonlit night set up; while I have the shimmering light, plus the silent twinkling of the stars, plus the distant sound of a piano fading in the silent scented air . . . It's excruciating. (*Pause.*) Yes, I'm coming more and more to the conclusion that it's not a question of forms, old or new, but of writing without thought to any forms at all – writing because it flows freely out of your heart.

Someone taps on the window nearest to the desk.

What was that? (*Looks out of the window.*) I can't see anything . . . (*Opens the glass door and looks into the garden.*) Someone running down the steps. (*Calls*) Who's there?

He goes out. He can be heard walking rapidly across the verandah. A moment later he comes back in with NINA.

Nina! Nina!

NINA *lays her head on his chest and sobs, trying to control herself.*

(*Moved*). Nina! Nina! It's you . . . it's you . . . I had a kind of premonition – my mind's been in a torment all day. (*Takes her hat and shawl.*) Oh, my dear girl, my love – she's come! We mustn't cry, we mustn't.

NINA. There's someone here.

KONSTANTIN. There's no one.

NINA. Lock the doors – someone may come in.

KONSTANTIN. No one's going to come in.

NINA. Your mother's here, I know. Lock the doors . . .

KONSTANTIN (*locks the righthand door with its key, then crosses to the lefthand door*). There's no lock on this one. I'll barricade it with the chair. (*Puts an armchair against the door.*) Don't worry, no one's going to come in now.

NINA (*gazes intently into his face*). Let me look at you. (*Looks round.*) It's warm in here, it's nice . . . This was the drawing-room then. Have I changed a lot?

KONSTANTIN. Yes, you have . . . You've lost weight, and

your eyes have got bigger. Nina, it's strange somehow to be seeing you. Why didn't you ever let me in? Why didn't you come sooner? I know you've been living here for almost a week . . . I've been coming every day, several times a day, and standing under your window like a beggar.

NINA. I was afraid you'd hate me. Every night I dream that you're looking at me and not recognising me. If only you knew what things had been like! I've been coming here from the moment I arrived . . . walking by the lake. I've been by your house many times, but I couldn't make up my mind to come in. Let's sit down.

They sit.

We'll sit and talk. Talk and talk. It's nice in here – it's warm, it's cosy . . . You hear the wind? It says in Turgenev somewhere: 'Lucky the man who on nights like these has a roof over his head and a warm corner.' I'm the seagull. No, that's not right. (*Rubs her forehead.*) What was I talking about? Oh, yes . . . Turgenev . . . 'And Lord help all homeless wanderers . . .' It's all right. (*Sobs.*)

KONSTANTIN. Nina, you're crying again . . . Nina!

NINA. It's all right – it's a relief . . . I haven't cried these two whole years. Then last night I went to look at the garden to see if our theatre was still there. And it is – it's been standing there all this time. I cried for the first time in two years, and I felt a weight lifting, I felt my heart clearing. You see? – I've stopped crying. (*Takes him by the hand.*) So, you've become a writer now . . . You're a writer – I'm an actress . . . We're launched upon the world, even us . . . I used to be full of joy in life, like a little child – I'd wake up in the morning and start singing – I loved you – I had dreams of glory . . . And now? First thing tomorrow morning I'm off to Yeletz – third class, with the peasants – and in Yeletz I shall have the more educated local businessmen pressing their attentions upon me. It's a rough trade, life!

KONSTANTIN. Why Yeletz?

NINA. I'm contracted for the entire winter season. It's time to be getting there.

KONSTANTIN. Nina, I've cursed you, I've hated you, I've torn up your letters and your photographs – but not a moment when I didn't know that I was bound to you, heart and soul, for all eternity. It's not within my power to cease loving you, Nina. From the moment I lost you and began to be published I've found my life unliveable – nothing but pain . . . It's as if my youth had suddenly been stripped from me – I feel I've been living in this world for ninety years. I say your name – I kiss the ground you've walked upon. Wherever I look I see your face – I see the tender smile that shone on me in the summer of my life . . .

NINA (*dismayed*). Why are you talking like this?

KONSTANTIN. I'm all alone. I've no one's affection to warm me – I'm as cold as the grave – and whatever I write, it's dry and stale and joyless. Stay here, Nina, I beg you, or else let me come with you!

NINA *quickly puts on her hat and shawl.*

KONSTANTIN. Nina, why? Nina, for the love of God . . .

He watches her put her things on. Pause.

NINA. My horses are at the gate. Don't come out – I'll find my own way . . . (*On the verge of tears.*) Give me some water.

KONSTANTIN (*gives her a drink of water*). Where are you going now?

NINA. Into town. (*Pause.*) Is your mother here?

KONSTANTIN. Yes, she is . . . Uncle was taken ill last Thursday and we wired her to come.

NINA. Why do you say you kissed the ground I walked upon? I ought to be put to death. (*Leans on the table.*) I'm so tired! If only I could rest . . . just rest! (*Raises her head.*) I'm the seagull . . . That's not right. I'm the actress. Yes!

Hears ARKADINA *and* TRIGORIN *laughing. Listens, then
runs to the lefthand door and looks through the keyhole.*

He's here, too . . . (*Crosses back to* KONSTANTIN.) Yes, of
course . . . Not that it matters . . . Of course, though . . . He
didn't believe in the theatre – he did nothing but laugh at my
ambitions – and gradually I stopped believing, too – I began
to lose heart . . . Then there were the burdens of love – the
jealousy, the perpetual anxiety for my little boy . . . I became
a paltry thing, a nonentity – my acting lost all meaning . . .
I didn't know what to do with my hands, I didn't know how
to stand, I couldn't control my voice. You don't understand
what it's like when you feel you're acting badly. I'm the
seagull. No, that's not right . . . Do you remember – you
shot a seagull? One day by chance a man comes along and sees
her. And quite idly he destroys her . . . An idea for a short
story . . . That's not right . . . (*Rubs her forehead.*) What was
I talking about . . .? Acting, yes . . . I'm not like that now
. . . I've become a real actress. I take pleasure in my
performance – I delight in it. I'm in a state of intoxication up
there – I feel I'm beautiful. And now, while I've been staying
here, I've kept walking round – walking and walking,
thinking and thinking – and I've had the feeling that with
every day my spiritual strength has grown . . . I know now,
Kostya, I understand now, that in our work – and it makes
no difference whether we're acting or whether we're
writing – the main thing is not the fame, not the glory, not
all the things I used to dream of; it's the ability to endure.
Learn to bear your cross; have faith. I have faith, and for me
the pain is less. And when I think about my vocation, I'm not
afraid of life.

KONSTANTIN (*sadly*). You've found your way – you know
where you're going. While I'm still floundering in a chaos of
dreams and images without knowing who or what it's all for.
I've no faith, nor any idea where my vocation lies.

NINA (*listens*). Sh . . . I'm going. Goodbye. When I've become a great actress come and see me perform. You promise? But now . . . (*Presses his hand.*) It's late. I can scarcely stand . . . I'm so tired, I'm so hungry . . .

KONSTANTIN. Stay here – I'll give you some supper . . .

NINA. No, no . . . Don't come out – I'll find my own way . . . The horses are close by . . . So she's brought him with her? Well, there we are – it makes no difference. Don't tell Trigorin anything when you see him . . . I love him. I love him even more than before . . . An idea for a short story . . . I love him; I love him passionately; I love him to the point of desperation. It was good before, Kostya! Do you remember? Such a bright, warm, joyous, innocent life. Such feelings. Feelings like graceful, delicate flowers . . . Do you remember? (*Recites.*) 'Men and lions, partridges and eagles, spiders, geese, and antlered stags, the unforthcoming fish that dwelt beneath the waters, starfish and creatures invisible to the naked eye; in short – all life, all life, all life, its dismal round concluded, has guttered out. Thousands of centuries have passed since any living creature walked the earth, and this poor moon in vain lights up her lantern. In the meadows the dawn cry of the crane is heard no more, and the May bugs are silent in the lime groves . . .'

Embraces KONSTANTIN *impulsively, and runs out through the glass door.*

KONSTANTIN (*after a pause*). Just so long as no one meets her in the garden and then tells Mama. It might distress Mama . . .

Over the next two minutes he silently tears up all his manuscripts and throws them under the desk, then opens the righthand door and goes out.

DORN (*off, trying to open the lefthand door*). Odd. The door seems to be locked . . .

He enters, and puts the armchair back in its place.

Obstacle race.

Enter ARKADINA *and* POLINA, *followed by* YAKOV, *bearing bottles and* MASHA, *then* SHAMRAYEV *and* TRIGORIN.

ARKADINA. Put the wine, and the beer for Boris Alekseyevich, on the table here. We're going to drink as we play. Do sit down, everyone.

POLINA (*to* YAKOV). Look sharp, now, and bring some tea as well. (*Lights the candles and sits down at the card-table.*)

SHAMRAYEV *takes* TRIGORIN *across to the cupboard.*

SHAMRAYEV. This is the thing I was telling you about earlier . . . (*Gets the stuffed seagull out of the cupboard.*) You asked me to have it done.

TRIGORIN (*looks at the seagull*). No recollection! (*After a moment's thought.*) No recollection!

A shot, off right. Everyone jumps.

ARKADINA (*alarmed*). What was that?

DORN. Nothing to worry about. Something in my medicine chest bursting, I expect. No cause for alarm.

He goes off through the righthand door, and a few moments later comes back in again.

Yes, that's what it was. A bottle of ether bursting. (*He hums to himself.*)

ARKADINA (*sitting down at the table*). Oh, it frightened me! It reminded me of the time when . . . (*Puts her hands over her face.*) I thought for a moment I was going to faint . . .

DORN (*leafing through a magazine; to* TRIGORIN). There was an article in here a couple of months back . . . From a correspondent in America, and I wanted to ask you, quite offhand . . . (*Puts an arm behind* TRIGORIN'*s back and leads him away downstage.*) . . . this being a question that very much interests me . . . (*Lowers his voice.*) Get her out of here, will you. The fact is, he's shot himself . . .

CURTAIN

Notes

Characters
Arkadina: see Translator's Introduction, p.lxxxvi. In the original cast list she is also given a Christian name and patronymic, Irina Nikolaevna (i.e. Irina, daughter of Nikolai) and, in the original play, is sometimes addressed formally with both.
Konstantin: Konstantin Gavrilovich in the original (Konstantin, son of Gabriel). In the play he is sometimes formally addressed by both Christian name and patronymic. Konstantin's surname is Treplev, with the stress on the first syllable. In critical studies of the play he is frequently referred to by his surname and, sometimes, you will find this has been stressed and transliterated incorrectly as Treplyov/Trepliov, with the stress on the last syllable. In the play he is also addressed by an affectionate diminutive of Konstantin, 'Kostya' (see Note on Pronunciation).
Sorin: identified as Petr (pronounced Piotr) Nikolaevich in the original.
Nina: Nina Mikhailovna Zarechnaia in the original (Nina, daughter of Mikhail Zarechnii) but although she is never formally addressed by her Christian name and patronymic in the original, she is sometimes referred to by her surname only. The name may be significant as it contains the meaning 'beyond the river'.
Shamrayev: Il'ia Afanas'evich in the original (Il'ia, son of Afanasi).
Polina: Polina Andreevna in the original (Polina, daughter of Andrei). In some translations her name is anglicised as Pauline.
Masha: she appears in her diminutive form in the original cast list but is referred to, at certain points in the play, as Maria Il'inichna (Maria, daughter of Il'ia).
Trigorin: Boris Alekseevich in the original (Boris, son of Aleksei). He is sometimes formally addressed by both name and patronymic. His professional occupation in Russian is taken from the French, 'a belletrist'. Some commentators suggest that the root of his name 'tri gory' (three mountains) has some significant meaning.
Dorn: Evgenii Sergeevich in the original (Evgenii, son of Sergei).
Medvedenko: Semen Semenovich in the original (pronounced Semion Semionovich). The fact that his name repeats that of his

father may be relevant to an understanding of his rather predictable character. The root of his name 'medved' means 'a bear'. He eventually marries Masha, which might remind Russian readers of a comic folk tale 'Masha and the Bear' (Masha i medved').

It emerges during the course of the play that Arkadina is 43, Sorin is 60, Dorn 55, Konstantin 25 and Masha 22. Trigorin is 'well short of forty' and is probably about twice Nina's age. All will have aged two years by the autumn of Act Four.

Act One

1 *I'm in mourning for my life*: the first of many intertextual references in the play. This line is spoken by a character in *Bel Ami*, a novel by the famous French short story writer Guy de Maupassant (1850–93) whose *Sur l'eau* is referred to at the beginning of Act Two.

Theoretically. In practice . . . : the distinctions between theory and practice in this play are like those between spirit and matter. The only person who talks about the relationship between the two in the course of the action is, ironically, the practically-minded Medvedenko.

A play written by Konstantin, and his Nina will be acting in it: in the original he says: 'Zarechnaia will be acting and the play has been written by Konstantin Gavrilovich.' It is interesting that Medvedenko refers to the amateur actress as if she had the professional stage name of someone like Arkadina. He also refers to Konstantin with a degree of formality.

2 *their souls . . . my soul*: Medvedenko's mode of speech shifts between the elevated and the prosaic. He is generally seen to be concerned with more utilitarian matters but here is clearly trying to appeal to Masha with his concern for 'higher things'. She brings matters down to earth by snorting snuff.

all I get from you is indifference: in the original, Medvedenko, as is his wont when seeking to impress, says 'all I get from you is indifferentism', which is a Russian neologism with suggestions of a loan word from English but, in any case, sounds pretentious.

Oh, fiddle: a favourite expression of Masha's which others also use throughout the play. In the original the word is 'pustyaki', the root of which is 'pust' and suggests emptiness and

nothingness (as in 'pustynia', a desert). Variant translations are
legion, from 'Nonsense' to 'Rubbish', to 'Don't be silly', to no
translation at all.

*it's a thousand times easier to go round in rags and beg your
bread than it is to . . .*: this is already Masha's second reference
to her preference for beggary and another of the play's many
leitmotifs.

No question about it [. . .] *when all's said and done*: Sorin's
discourse is interspersed with meaninglessly repetitive
expressions such as the above. His references to sleep and
dream also introduce another leitmotif.

I feel as if a horse and cart had gone over me: 'Ia ves' pazbit'
(I'm all smashed up /completely shattered). No horses or carts
in the original.

3 *And would you mind . . . ?*: in the original Sorin begins his
question by addressing Masha formally as Maria Il'inichna.

from the moment you arrived you'd want to be away again: at
the end of this sentence Chekhov has the stage direction '(*He
laughs*)' followed by Sorin's saying 'I always felt pleased to get
away from here . . .'

If Nina's late: in the original, Konstantin, like Medvedenko
earlier, refers to her as 'Zarechnaia', rather than Nina. Later,
although he addresses her as 'Nina', both address each other
formally as 'you' (vy) and never use the more intimate 'thou'
(ty).

4 *in case her novelist takes a fancy to Nina*: this line is from an
earlier draft of the play. Most versions have Chekhov's
subsequent alteration '. . . because she's not in it [i.e. his play]
but Nina is'.

Nekrasov: N.A. Nekrasov (1821–78) a civic poet with a social
conscience as well as a famous editor. His work tended to
idealise the Russian peasantry, which makes Arkadina's
apparent enthusiasm for his poetry seem a conscious piece of
Chekhovian irony.

Duse: Eleonora Duse, a famous Italian actress (1859–1924).

La Dame aux Camélias, or whatever: in the original it is '*La
Dame aux Camélias* and *Chad Zhizni*' (The Fumes of Life).
The latter is a reworking, by Boleslav Markevich, of his
scandalous novel of low life, *The Abyss*, staged under the title

Olga Rantseva at the Alexandrinsky Theatre, St Petersburg, in 1888. Chekhov disliked this kind of writing which he described as being 'written with a broom'. *The Lady of the Camelias* was a novel by Alexandre Dumas *fils* which he adapted as a play, *Camille*, and which Verdi turned into an opera, *La Traviata*.

she's afraid of three candles: the following explanations are offered in their notes to translations of the play. According to George Calderon, in Russia three candles are put by a dead body, two at the head and one at the feet. According to Eugene Bristow, this refers to a fairly widespread superstition: if three lights (be they candles, lamps, or torches) are burning, one must be snuffed out; otherwise, misfortune will occur; moreover, this practice is especially observed by actors.

She's got seventy thousand roubles sitting in a bank in Odessa: this is a large sum of money in late-nineteenth-century terms. It could be part of an inheritance, or a settlement, or it could be an indication that Arkadina is a very successful and well-paid actress. Odessa was the most significant Black Sea port in tsarist Russia, known as Russia's 'Marseilles'.

5 *(pulling the petals off a flower)*: Chekhov is said to have had a pantheistic streak in him and certainly had passionate ecological concerns. According to F.L. Lucas, he also shared the compassionate dislike of someone like Walter Savage Landor for picking live flowers.

they attempt to extract a moral: Chekhov uses the verb *vyudit'* (to fish out) for 'extract', which may have intentional connections with Trigorin's favourite pastime.

just as Maupassant ran from the sight of the Eiffel Tower: Guy de Maupassant describes this feeling in his autobiographical *La Vie errante*.

But then she smokes, she drinks, she quite openly lives with that novelist: this is from the censored original version of the play. Chekhov subsequently amended the line to 'ona vedet bestolkovuiu zhizn' (she lives a senseless/pointless life).

they're always bandying her name about: Chekhov uses the third person plural of the verb *trepat'* – 'trepliut' for 'bandying about', which sounds like Konstantin's surname and Arkadina's married name.

6 *owing to circumstances beyond the editor's control*: this phrase

would normally refer to state censorship; here the implication is that Konstantin has been kicked out of university, but for what reasons is not clear (see Note on the Translation, p.xcv).

a Kiev shopkeeper: 'Kievskii meshchanin', which can mean a member of the merchant class, or a member of the bourgeoisie. Kiev, situated on the river Dnieper, was the capital of Ancient Russia and an important religious centre. It is now the capital of the Ukraine.

Tolstoy or Zola: Leo Tolstoy (1828–1910) Russian novelist, author of *War and Peace* and *Anna Karenina*, and Emile Zola (1840–1902), French novelist, author of *Germinal* and a key figure in the Naturalist movement.

7 *I kept whipping and whipping the horse*: 'Ia gnala loshad, gnala' (I was urging and urging the horse), which does not necessarily require the whip.

(Goes off right singing Schumann's 'Two Grenadiers'): the source of the song, opus 49 no.1 by Robert Schumann (1810–56), is not given in the original where Sorin simply leaves singing 'Vo Frantsii dva grenadera . . .' (In France two grenadiers . . .). The words of the song are a poem, *Die beiden Grenadiere*, by Heinrich Heine (1797–1856). A grenadier was originally a soldier who threw grenades; later the term was reserved for a company of the finest and tallest men. The poem consists of a conversation between two French grenadiers who have returned to Europe after being captured in Russia in 1812 and who are bewailing the defeat and capture of Napoleon after Waterloo. They vow to rise from their own graves to continue to fight for him. The key verse, as far as the play is concerned, is the fifth where the conflict between the real and the ideal is treated ironically: 'To hell with wife, to hell with child, / my thoughts are for things far higher; / let them beg, if they've nothing to eat – / my Emperor, my Emperor captured!' Napoleon is, of course, one quarter of the world soul in Konstantin's play.

deputy prosecutors: George Calderon, the first English translator of *The Seagull*, provides a note for his own translation which glosses 'deputy prosecutor' as 'Assistant Procureur': 'Some cheeky junior of forty. Sorin's career has been passed among Procureurs and Assistant Procureurs, a special breed of prosecuting counsel attached to the Ministry of Justice. He has worked his way up to the dignity of Over-Procureur, with the title of Actual State Councillor, on a level with Major-Generals and Rear-Admirals according to Peter the Great's Table of Comparative Precedence.' In the first version of the play Sorin referred at one point to a paper which he wrote and which gave him great satisfaction on the efficacy of trial by jury. Whether he was in favour or against it isn't clear.

My heart's full of you: Nina uses the plural at this point. She does not just mean Konstantin but 'all of you' or 'of you all'.

8 *Sir*: in this translation, in answer to Konstantin's questions, Yakov twice answers 'Sir'. In the original he says 'Tochno tak', which does not necessarily imply subservience but is something like 'Just so' or 'That's right' or 'Right you are'.

just a kind of recitation: 'chitka' in the original, is a read-through at the rehearsal stage.

9 *Dorn hums*: see A Note on the Translation, p.xciv. In the original he sings a specific melody with the following words 'Ne govori, chto molodost' sgubila . . .' (Say not that your youth's been ruined . . .). The words are taken from Nekrasov and might be said to have significance for the play as a whole, especially as it affects the fate of the young people.

Wrapped up in your conversation with her: 'with Irina Nikolaevna' in the original.

Oh, fiddle: Polina repeats Masha's expression 'pustiaki'. Daughter presumably picked it up from mother.

Dorn (hums): on this occasion the words are 'Ia vnov' pered toboiu . . .' (Once again before thee. [I stand enchanted]). The line is taken from a love song by V. Kradin. Dorn repeats the line, plus the bit in square brackets, at the end of the play.

10 *Poltava*: a town in the Ukraine and the site of a famous battle between Peter the Great and the Swedes which was the subject of a famous poem by Pushkin.

Chadin . . . Krechinsky's Wedding . . . Sadovsky: 'Chadin, Pavel Semenich' in the original, which seems to be an invented name. *Krechinsky's Wedding* is the first part of a trilogy by the nineteenth-century playwright Sukhovo-Kobylin. Prov Mikhailovich Sadovsky was a member of a famous Russian acting family and noted for his portrayal of Raspluiev, a miserly villain in *Krechinsky's Wedding*.

De gustibus aut bene aut nihil: Shamrayev confuses two Latin expressions – 'De gustibus non est disputandum' (There's no disputing matters of taste) and 'De mortuis aut bene aut nihil' (If you can't speak well of the dead, say nothing).

my precious: 'Moi milyi syn ...' (My dear son ...) in the original.

'Come hither, my dear Hamlet ... the nasty sty ...': the exchange of lines from *Hamlet* is taken by Chekhov from N.A. Polevoi's 1837 translation (Act III, Sc. IV, ll.88–93). The exchange, which is in prose not verse in Russian, runs in literal translation as follows: 'ARKADINA: My son! You've turned my eyes into my soul and I have seen there such bloody and such deadly sores – there's no salvation. KONSTANTIN: And why did you give yourself to vice and seek love in the abyss of crime?' As it is important for an audience to recognise the quotation, it probably needs to be in the original for English audiences and in whatever translation of Hamlet is most recognisable to foreign audiences. However, Hamlet's reply to his mother in Polevoi's version bears little resemblance to the verbal savagery of Shakespeare's original, and English translators have sometimes inserted a tamer line from elsewhere in *Hamlet* at this point.

A horn sounds behind the improvised stage: a 'rozhok', which is probably a ram's horn. In a poem by Viacheslav Ivanov called 'The Alpine Horn' (1901) nature is described as a symbolic horn which resounds to make an echo – the echo being God.

11 *this poor moon*: this is probably a misprint for 'pale' as the words for 'poor' and 'pale' in Russian are very similar (bedny/ bledny). Recent Russian scholarship based on the original manuscript of the play suggests that the appearance of a handwritten 'bledny' (pale), at one point, would seem to indicate that the printed 'bedny' (poor) is a mistake. Chekhov was a fan of Bal'mont who was Shelley's Russian translator and in whose famous poem the moon is 'pale for weariness'. *In me are the souls*: feminists will note that the world soul consists mainly of strong masculine leaders, despite the sex of the speaker. The onomatopoeia of 'least of leeches' is there in the original 'poslednei piavki', minus the assonance.

Decadent School: see Commentary, p.xxiv.

Mama!: see note on pronunciation. Diminutives of this sort are notoriously difficult to translate. The English 'Mum', 'Mummy' or 'Mamma' (the last of which would be stressed on the second syllable) sound quite wrong. Here, the translation has stuck to the Russian with the stress on the first syllable; translators usually try to get round the problem by deploying the neutral, and more formal, 'Mother'.

12 *bright Sirius*: the dog-star, in the constellation of the Greater Dog, the brightest of the fixed stars.

13 *a skit*: 'shutka' in the original, literally 'a joke'. Chekhov called his one-act plays 'shutki'.

14 *Jupiter wroth means Jupiter wrong*: 'You are angry, Jupiter . . .' in the original. Jupiter was the principal Roman deity, the equivalent of the Greek Zeus whose weapon was the thunderbolt.

the leading actor: Arkadina uses French in the original, calling the doctor the 'jeune premier' and referring to him as 'Doctor Evgenii Sergeevich'.

16 *he just wishes the earth would swallow him up*: the idiom is not so expressive in the original which suggests that Trigorin tends to collapse in a heap – 'on provalivaetsia'.

with malice aforethought: 'kak narochno' might equally well mean 'as ill-luck would have it'. It is not so apparent that this was a 'set-up'.

the bass from our church choir: 'bas iz nashikh sinodal'nykh pevchikh' (a bass from our synod choir), i.e. a member of the choir founded in 1892 under the direction of the Holy Synod to serve two of the principal churches in the Kremlin, to sing in religious street processions in Moscow etc. (Calderon).

(*In a deep but insubstantial bass.*): the words 'but insubstantial' have been added in the present translation. Apparently this is one of those apocryphal stories which are almost part of Russian folklore. The fact that Shamrayev repeats it as if it were true may be the source of the 'embarrassed' silence which follows; or it may just be a response to the utter inconsequentiality of the tale.

A quiet angel flew past: 'tikhii angel proletel', a common Russian expression when a group becomes aware of a long silence since the last person spoke.

my pet: 'moia kroshka' (literally 'my crumb'), a term of
endearment used to children and implying something tiny.

Act Two

20 *Dorn quietly sings*: the source of the aria is not identified in the
original where Dorn 'quietly sings' the line 'Rasskazhite vy ei,
tsvety moi . . .' (Tell her, my flowers . . .). Siebel is a village
youth in Gounod's opera *Faust*, in love with Marguerite and
who, at this point in Act Three, has entered her garden to pick
some flowers for her but, before doing so, sings 'Faites-lui mes
aveux . . .' ('Bear my avowel to her . . .', which in Russian is
rendered as 'Tell her, my flowers . . .'). When he picks the
flowers they shrivel in his hand as Mephistopheles had
predicted. He then spies a font of holy water into which he dips
his finger whereupon, at a touch, the flowers cease to shrivel.
He places the bouquet on the steps of the house for Marguerite
to find, which Mephistopheles then replaces with a casket of
jewels and a handsome bouquet from Faust, whom
Mephistopheles then helps to seduce Marguerite. The
significance of flowers in *The Seagull* constitutes another
leitmotif, as does seduction.

comme il faut: in French in the original.

21 *gone into town*: this suggests only a short journey. In the
original, they have gone to Tver, an old Russian town north-
west of Moscow which, depending on where the action of the
play is set, could be miles away and hence account for the three
days' absence.

22 *it will bring bad luck*: the verb 'sglazit' can mean to put one off
by overpraising. George Calderon suggests that its other
meaning applies here: to 'bewitch', in the sense of exercising
the power of the Evil Eye over Nina through arousal of others'
envy.

Maupassant . . . 'On the Water': as a short story writer himself,
Chekhov was very aware of the figure of Maupassant. The
influence of his *Sur l'eau* on *The Seagull* is explained by Jerome
H. Katsell (in Barricelli: 1981, pp.18–34), where he points to
thematic and situational parallels including the 'art versus
nature' theme as well as themes of freedom and the artistic

personality.

please – read a bit of his play!: this is an invitation to 'recite' rather than 'read'. In the first performance, Nina repeated some lines from the play at this point but, because of the laughter which accompanied this and which erupted again when sections of the play were repeated in Act Four, Chekhov agreed that this first repetition be cut.

Valerian drops: the nineteenth-century equivalent of something like valium, a form of tranquilliser.

23 *Oh, pish, you old civil servant*: 'Pustoe, vashe prevoskhoditelstvo.' Dorn uses the term by which Sorin would probably have been addressed by his inferiors, something like 'Your Most High Excellency'. His 'pustoe' echoes Sorin's earlier 'pustiaki'.

You can't expect a beggar to be happy: Sorin's reference to beggars and 'having one's fill in life', with the sense of being over-gorged (syt po gorlo) adds another dimension to this particular leitmotif of beggary – being 'full' or being 'empty' having both literal and more abstract connotations.

25 *Trigorin with his fishing-rods and buckets*: when asked by an actor at the Moscow Art Theatre which aspects of Trigorin were important, Chekhov gave no hint as to his psychological or emotional life but said he wore checked trousers, that his shoes were down at heel and, most especially, he made his own fishing-rods. Fishing, as a symbolically displaced activity, has a long psychological history.

26 *Merci bien*: in French in the original.

27 *despised the common herd*: 'preziraet tolpu' (despise the crowd) is not quite so contemptuous in the original. The word 'tolpa' (crowd) later reminds Dorn of the world soul (in Act Four).

Enter Konstantin, hatless: students might like to speculate as to why Chekhov requires that Konstantin be 'hatless' at this point.

What does that signify?: perhaps this makes Nina a rather too self-conscious semiotician. 'Chto eto znachit?' in the original, 'What does this mean?'

I had the dishonour: 'Ia imel podlost' . . .' in the original. There may be some verbal self-consciousness on Konstantin's part here – playing with the opposite to the normal expression 'Ia imel chest . . .' (I had the honour).

28 *I burnt it, every last torn-up shred of it*: in the 1898 Art Theatre production, Meyerhold, who played Konstantin, was shown tearing up and burning his other manuscripts at the end of Act Four, which Chekhov does not ask for, but the directors were plainly recalling the fate of his first manuscript.

Words, words, words: Hamlet's reply to Polonius when the latter asks him what he is reading (Act II, Sc.II, ll.191–2).

29 *what sort of creature you were*: 'shto vy za shtuchka' (what sort of thing you are). The phrase has a somewhat indulgent, patronising air. A 'shtuchka' is usually something inanimate.

(After a moment's reflection): in the original, Chekhov prefaces the next line with 'It's one of two things' and then: 'Either you have . . .' etc.

idées fixes: not in French in the original which has 'nasilstvennye predstavleniia' (powerful impressions). Note how Trigorin goes on to deny the sunlit nature of his life by reference to the moon and that the 'days and nights' in which he can only think of the moon is the title of one of his books. A good deal of this speech also seems to owe a debt to Maupassant's *Sur l'eau* where a novelist is described as nibbling, stealing and exploiting everything he lays eyes on.

30 *I see that cloud up there, looking like a grand piano*: there may be an echo here of Hamlet's asking Polonius to contemplate a cloud in the shape of a camel (Act III, Sc.II, l.368).

I make a rapid mental note: 'skoree motaiu na us', literally 'twirl it into my moustache'. The Russian expression means 'to listen intently to a conversation, without contributing to it, and remember all that has been said for some future occasion'. (Henry: 1965, p.115).

I catch us both up: Trigorin uses the verb 'lovit', which is also used for fishing; 'lovit' rybu' (to catch a fish).

I'm picking the flowers themselves and trampling on their roots: another extension of the flower leitmotif.

31 *like the wretched clerk in that story of Gogol's*: the minor civil servant, Poprishchin, in one of Gogol's 'Petersburg Tales', *Diary of a Madman* (1836), who imagines overhearing conversations between dogs and ends up in a lunatic asylum

imagining himself to be the King of Spain.

dark hair [. . .] *fair hair*: in Act Four, Trigorin conveys the feelings of an intrigued reading public in Konstantin's pseudonymous identity by relaying their curiosity as to whether he is dark or fair-headed, which is about as relevant to literary appreciation as knowing whether the author of *Hamlet* was bald or wore a wig.

Turgenev's 'Fathers and Children': 'Otsy i deti' sometimes translated as 'Fathers and Sons', Ivan Turgenev's 1862 novel about a clash between the generations.

32 *I love the common people*: a sentiment Nina does not seem to share. In Act Four she speaks disparagingly of having to travel third class with peasants.

Agamemnon: commander of the Greek army which besieged Troy.

33 *And quite idly he destroys her, like this seagull*: in Chekhov's first version of the play he had Nina say at this point '(*with a shudder*) Please, don't . . .', implying her self-conscious identification with the fate of the fictional heroine. But he cut the line and inserted a pause instead.

Act Three

It emerges, during the course of the act, that a week has passed since the end of Act Two.

34 *to tear this love out of my heart . . . by the roots*: the association between hearts and flowers in the play is a fairly obvious one.

35 *I've only got one bean in my hand*: Nina is holding a single pea (goroshina) in the original. The alteration has perhaps been made because 'one pea' can sound like '1p' to English ears.

36 *Remember me sometimes*: Masha has already asked Trigorin to be remembered by him. Perhaps this is another *Hamlet* reference – to the moment when the ghost of Hamlet's father asks to be remembered. When characters leave at the end of Act Three, there is a spate of requests to be remembered.

Pardon: in French in the original and clearly meant ironically.

Page 121, lines 11 and 12: as if the quotation were not significant enough, Nina seems to have selected 'significant' page and line numbers which are an anagram of each other.

37 *the new government building*: 'zemstvo' in the original. The
zemstvos were rural councils set up after the emancipation of
the serfs in 1861 and the land reforms of 1864.

stuck here like a gudgeon in the mud: see A Note on the
Translation, pp.xciii–xciv.

Maybe he should get a job: 'na sluzhbu' would normally imply
a civil service post or joining the military.

39 *There's a riddle*: the riddle posed Oedipus by the Sphinx, 'What
goes on four legs in the morning, two at midday and three in
the evening?' to which he gave the correct answer – 'Man'.
Sorin is at the 'in the evening on three' stage, as he walks with a
stick.

if you had a sudden attack of generosity: Konstantin is as
generous with his mother's money vis-à-vis his uncle as his
uncle was earlier vis-à-vis his nephew.

He promised to be here at ten: possibly an indication of how
seriously Dorn takes Konstantin's suicide attempt; after all, it is
difficult to point a gun at your temple and *miss*. Or it may be a
comment on the kind of negligent doctor Dorn has become.

You're not going to start playing with guns again: the term for
'playing with guns' here is 'delaesh chik-chik', which might be
translated as 'Now you're not going to go playing click-click
again are you?' The term suggests the noise of cocking a gun
and pulling the trigger but the tone Arkadina adopts is of the
kind used when talking to small boys at play.

40 *You were still working in the State theatre*: if this is the case,
then Arkadina's present role as a provincial actress would
represent a bit of a come-down. The most prestigious posts
were those held at the Imperial [State] Theatres of St
Petersburg and Moscow, either the Alexandrinsky or the
Maly, where Russia's finest actors were employed.

Surely you remember? . . . two ballet dancers: it is perhaps
typical of Arkadina to remember the trivial and forget the
important. It is clear from the original that the ballet dancers in
question are female (baleriny) as ballet dancers can equally be
male; moreover they are 'religious' female ballet dancers, not
quite dancing nuns but this might have some bearing on an

audience's perception of Nina's seeming to combine religious
faith with acting (in Act Four).

41 *You couldn't write so much as a miserable farce!*: 'a
vaudeville' in the original, not our sense of music-hall or the
more raucous American variety, but a more genteel and frothy
light comedy with songs imported into Russia from France and
very popular during the nineteenth century.

42 *Konstantin picks up the bandage from the floor*: this could be
seen as a comment on Trigorin's previous line and Nina's
apparent offer of her life, as a soiled object to be snatched up.

43 *I feel as if a voice were calling me to her!*: 'menyia manit k nei'
contains a real sense of Trigorin having left the world of
literary realism for otherworldly symbolist realms towards
which he is being enticed by ethereal creatures having sloughed
off the 'material envelope' of worldly flesh (in Dorn's words). It
is as if John Galsworthy had metamorphosed into W.B. Yeats
and prepares us for the world of 'poetry' and 'dreams' which he
is about to describe to Arkadina, which also extends the
leitmotif of 'sleep' and 'dream'. The 'realism' of Arkadina's
emotional and physical appeal which follows is in obvious
comic contrast to this escapist fantasy. Notice that Arkadina
also uses the appeal of an art form – crude melodrama – to win
him over.

44 *incense at your altar*: 'Ty dumaesh, eto fimiam?' (Do you think
this is just flattery?) 'Fimiam' literally means incense but here is
being used metaphorically. The translation manages to turn the
literal Russian into a uniquely English metaphorical expression.
Now he's mine: more like the melodramatic 'aside' a
moustachioed villain might deliver once a 'fair maid' had been
brought to the brink of capitulation.
Virgins' forest: 'Devichii bor' could also be translated as 'The
Maiden's Bush', which might have salacious significance in
view of what happens to Nina.

45 *I have to inform you*: Shamrayev begins his line with 'I have the
honour to inform you . . .' His expression of regret might be to
do with their leaving; it might equally well be regret at having
to let them have use of his precious horses.
Suzdaltzev . . . The Great Mail Robbery . . . Izmailov: the

actors' names seem to be invented ones; the play is a melodrama by F.A. Burdin (1830). In the original, Shamrayev also mentions that Izmailov was working in Elizavetgrad, which is a large town in the Ukraine.

Trats in a rap: the confusion is between 'My popali v zapadniu' (We've fallen into a trap) and 'My popali v zapandiu' (which is nonsense). Translators have had fun with this, perhaps one of the best versions being 'caught in a trap/trapped in a court' and the less happy 'caught in a trap/taught in a cap'. A cruder, more recent, version has 'caught in a trap/caught in a crap'. 'Raps in a trat' might also serve here.

46 *Inverness*: 'pal'to s pelerinoi' (a coat with a cape). An Inverness is a heavy, cloak-type garment reinforced over the shoulder area with a layer of cape.

if we're spared: this expression has a degree of comic pathos. The original has 'esli budem zhivy i zdorovy' (if we're alive and well).

Here, a ruble. That's for all three of you: about the equivalent of two shillings at the time (10 pence in today's currency, though two shillings was worth much more in the 1890s) – in other words, very mean. It is ironic, in the circumstances, that Arkadina asks to be remembered 'kindly'. She promptly forgets Polina's kindness in having brought the plums and leaves them behind, just before Trigorin 'forgets' his stick for which he returns (but this may be a mere ploy to see Nina).

47 *I'm going on the stage*: in the original, where the preceding dash is here, Nina says 'zhrebii broshen' (the die is cast), which continues the sense of chance and fate which her 'odd or even' game with Trigorin had introduced.

Slavyansky Bazar: one of the best hotels and restaurants in Moscow and the venue for the conversation between Stanislavsky and Nemirovich-Danchenko in 1897, which lasted nearly 24 hours and led to the founding of the Moscow Art Theatre. It is interesting that Trigorin suggests Nina put up at an expensive venue; his and Arkadina's lodgings seem to be less salubrious on the face of it.

Act Four

48 *Two years have elapsed*: as the play is in four acts, productions tend to place the interval after Act Two. However, recent critics have been struck by the greater effectiveness (and appropriateness) of placing the interval after Act Three.

The sound of the watchman's rattle: English readers, especially football fans, might think this is an implement twirled by hand emitting the familiar rasping explosion of sound. In fact, the implement in question is more like a clapper board, shaped like a large table-tennis bat with a piece of wood hinged laterally across its surface. A wave of the bat produces a 'clunk', or a 'double-clunk', according to the number of waves. The watchman would be one of the estate employees and the effect of the noise would be to warn intruders, or thieves, of a patrolling presence.

Masha (calls): in the original she calls 'Konstantin Gavrilovich!' twice and twice asks where 'Kostya' is.

It's as hideous as bare bones: 'Stoit golyi, bezobraznyi, kak skelet . . .' (literally, 'It stands naked, disgraceful, like a skeleton . . .'). Together with the storm outside, this image would appear to operate as some kind of external, expressionist modifier of the seemingly secure, warm world of interior action. The repetition of 'Kostya' here might also serve as an echo, to the Russian ear, of the word for a bare bone, 'kost'.

50 *be a bit kinder to my Masha*: no sooner has her daughter's husband turned his back than Polina seems to act as a kind of procuress, like Polonius in *Hamlet*, 'loosing' her daughter to Konstantin.

51 *You've got plenty of money*: 'Deneg u vas kury ne kliuiut' (literally, 'Your money isn't pecked away by hens'). There is a sense in which Medvedenko's life is dominated by the women who surround him to the extent that his 'henpecked' status is very real.

In thirty years of practice . . . night and day: Dorn's lament for the life of a typical doctor begins to sound like Trigorin's for the lot of the writer, whilst his 'day and night' reference also echoes Trigorin.

52 *Dorn hums to himself*: the actual words he sings at this point are 'Mesiats plyvet po nochnym nebesam' (The harvest moon

floats in the night skies) which is the first line of 'Tigrenok' (The Tiger Cub), a serenade which was 'popular throughout Europe with its theme of desperate and destructive love' (Rayfield: 1999, p.142) and which was composed by K.S. Shilovskii (1849–93).

The Man who wanted to: 'Chelovek, kotoryi khotel' which, in the original, Sorin promptly repeats in French translation, 'L'homme, qui a voulu'.

It's like talking to the gatepost: 'eto legomyslie' (that's mere flippancy) in the original.

You speak as someone who's eaten his fill: A leitmotif which, throughout, equates life and eating. If you look back to p.2 and Masha's line: 'You seem to think the worst thing that can happen to anyone is poverty, but I think it's a thousand times easier to go round in rags and beg your bread than it is to . . . Well you wouldn't understand.' The missing words would logically seem to be 'have a full stomach' or 'have plenty to eat', although she is referring to her own *feelings* at this point.

53 *There's a splendid street life there*: 'Tam prevoskhodnaia ulichnaia tolpa' (There's a splendid street crowd there). Dorn uses the word 'tolpa' (crowd) twice in this speech which goes on to privilege 'aimlessness', although his advice to Konstantin consists in his needing an 'aim' and a 'direction'.

54 *but she played them crudely and vulgarly, with a lot of howling and sawing of the air*: the translation here seems conscious of Hamlet's advice to the players not 'to saw the air' with their hands and may be relevant to the kind of performance Nina gives in Act Four.

like that play of Pushkin's: Paul Schmidt comments: 'In addition to *Hamlet*, another play [dramatic poem] whose action parallels the plot of *The Seagull* is *The Water Nymph* *(Rusalka)* by Alexander Sergeyevich Pushkin (1799–1837), Russia's foremost poet. Educated Russians would be as familiar with his work as we are with that of Shakespeare. *The Water Nymph* was written between 1829 and 1832, and was left unfinished [but] is about a young girl, a miller's daughter, who lives by the shore of a river and is seduced, made pregnant, and abandoned by a passing prince.' *The Plays of Anton Chekhov*, trans. Paul Schmidt (New York: Harper

Flamingo, 1998, pp.163–4). The heroine throws herself into the river Dnieper and is transformed into a 'rusalka', as a consequence of which her father goes mad with grief, imagining himself transformed into a crow.

55 *You old rake*: 'Staryilovelas' (You old Lovelace). Educated Russians were very familiar with the character of the rake Lovelace in Samuel Richardson's eighteenth-century novel *Clarissa*, to the extent that his name became a by-word for a seducer (with a pun on 'loveless' in English).

a little weather-beaten: 'vyvetrivaemsia pod vlianiem stikhii' (weathered under the influence of the elements). A reminder of the wild natural world outside and its relativising effect on the sheltered security of those indoors.

You're tempting fortune again: the verb is 'sglazit' in the original (Vy opiat' khotite sglazit' menyia) which can also mean 'You won't get round me with flattery on this occasion' ('sglazit', to put off by over-praising).

56 *are you fair or are you dark?*: this recalls Trigorin's anxiety about the arbitrary reception of his plays seeming to depend on the colour of the audience member's hair (p.31).

the Man in the Iron Mask: was the subject of a great number of literary works and historical studies. He was a prisoner of state in the reign of Louis XIV whose identity was a closely guarded secret and shrouded in mystery. He was variously believed to have been, amongst other possibilities, the Duke of Beaufort, the Duke of Buckingham, even Louis's own natural son. In fact, he was Mattioli, a minister of Duke Ferdinand of Mantua. Kept in various prisons over a long period, he eventually died in the Bastille in 1703 (Henry: 1965, pp.118–19).

No, I'm leaving for Moscow tomorrow: in the circumstances, it seems odd for Trigorin to come all this way for one night and may simply be Chekhov's device to ensure that the entire cast is assembled for the final act. It may also, however, suggest the kind of hold that Arkadina has over him in that he is at her beck and call.

a lotto set: lotto is a game like bingo. Each player is issued with a small playing board which has three horizontal rows of nine spaces each. Four spaces in each row are blank and the other five are marked with numbers up to 90. Each player puts a certain sum in the 'bank' and one player acts as banker (in this case, Masha) who draws small ivory markers from a bag. The banker calls out each number as it is drawn and each player covers the number if it appears on their board. When a player completes one covered row, he or she calls out 'Lotto' and wins the money in the bank (Schmidt, op. cit., p.163).

I've been developing an idea for a story: this may well be the story, the first inklings of which emerged at the end of Act Two and which featured someone like Nina, hence the need for Trigorin to refresh his memory of the scene of her outdoor performance. Her fate in the interim would certainly seem to have qualified her for the role of central figure in the story.

57 *He's not a general*: the sense here is that Medvedenko is not as important as a general, who would normally ride in a carriage or on horseback. It could otherwise mean that he is not as weak as a general, who needs a carriage, or a horse and is otherwise incapable of walking any distance without assistance.

Let's not waste time: Polina's sense of what it means to waste time here needs to be compared with her earlier recognition that our time is running out (p.45).

She gives everyone three cards each: the norm is one playing board per person but as in this instance the number of cards (small playing boards) exceeds the number of players, each gets three, otherwise many of the numbers called would be those on boards which had not been distributed, with resulting confusion.

He hasn't even cut the pages of mine: some publishers, for example in Norway, still produce editions of books where the individual leaves are not separated but have to be cut at the top and at the sides in order to read each page. So-called 'paper knives' were specially manufactured for this purpose.

58 *Kharkov*: a large city in the north-eastern part of the Ukraine.

They're being very rude about him in the papers: Trigorin has previously relayed Konstantin's readership's response to his mysterious authorial persona but said nothing about his critical reception. Shamrayev's comment suggests that reception of his work by literary critics has been hostile.

Never a single living character: Trigorin is echoing Nina's objection to Konstantin's play in Act One. The irony may be at

Trigorin's expense in that he (and others) imagine themselves to be 'characters' and 'alive' in an unproblematic sense which the play seeks to problematise.

60 *He has the neck of a broken bottle glittering on the bank of the millpool*: the image is used by Chekhov himself in his short story 'Volk' (The Wolf), 1886. In the same year he also mentioned this literary technique in a letter to his brother Alexander of 10 May.

61 *flows freely out of your heart*: 'from the soul' in the original (iz ego dushi).

   (Takes her hat and shawl): Laurence Senelick makes the point that the shawl is a 'tal'ma' in Russian, i.e. it is named after the French tragic actor François Joseph Talma (1763–1826) and thus has very specific theatrical and tragic connotations.

62 *standing under your window like a beggar*: this mention of beggary seems like a repetition of the image in Act One: 'I'll stand in the garden all night and look up at your window' (p.8).

   It says in Turgenev: in the 'Epilogue' to his novella *Rudin*, about a 'superfluous man' who, throughout the story, has been a Hamlet figure who cannot make up his mind, but who has metamorphosed into a Don Quixote in the last paragraph and perishes on the Paris barricades in 1848. The moment Nina is referring to runs: 'But outside the wind had risen and was howling with angry moans, violently shaking and rattling the window-panes. The long autumn night set in. It is good on such a night to be sitting under a roof at home, to have some warm corner ... And may God help all homeless wanderers' (trans. Richard Hare).

   I'm the seagull. No, that's not right: 'Ia – chaika ... Net, ne to.' Paul Schmidt suggests that the line she repeats in this scene, 'Net ne to' (No, that's not right), is a quotation from Pushkin's *Rusalka* and that some of her other lines in this scene paraphrase Pushkin's work (Schmidt, op. cit., pp.163–4).

   Yeletz: an old town in Lipetsk province in Southern Russia.

63 *Why are you talking like this?*: 'Zachem on tak govorit?' (Why is he talking like this? Like Trigorin earlier, in moments of emotional agitation, Nina addresses an unseen audience and refers to the other person on stage in the third person. Earlier

Trigorin had said in Arkadina's presence 'She doesn't understand! She won't understand!' (p.43).

I'm as cold as the grave: 'mne kholodno, kak v podzemel'e' (literally, 'I'm as cold as if in a vault/dungeon/underground cave'), with a sense of space, cold air and of being buried alive.

64   *Hears Arkadina and Trigorin laughing*: Chekhov often places laughter in counterpoint to serious sentiment (see the opening of *Three Sisters* where the laughter of the officers comments, in counterpoint, on the sisters' optimism).

looks through the keyhole: Chekhov might be commenting, in a play which is concerned with 'new forms', on 'keyhole' naturalism – i.e. a slice of life presented as if those enacting it were unaware of being observed, otherwise known as 'fourth wall' naturalism with the audience as 'eavesdroppers'. This moment is followed by her reference to Trigorin's disbelief in the theatre which, in turn, sparked her own disbelief.

I became a paltry thing, a nonentity: Konstantin's worst fear has also become Nina's, but this fear may be said to be predicated on the idea of *personal* significance, which both Chekhov's play (and Konstantin's idea of a world soul) would seem to question.

without knowing who or what it's all for: perhaps here lies the key to Konstantin's problem, one which lies at the heart of Tolstoy's 'What is Art?'. If art is the product of a narrow social group and is simply consumed by them without any reference to, or meaning for, the people at large, (the 'narod' or 'tolpa'), what purpose does it serve?

65   *Nina (listens)*: ironically, Nina has *not* been listening to Konstantin uttering what is possibly the most important sentiment in the play, but has been attending to events offstage. She peremptorily tells Konstantin to 'shoosh' whilst she gauges the significance of offstage noises which suggest that supper is over and her presence about to be discovered. It would seem to be Trigorin and Arkadina who are uppermost in her mind, not Konstantin.

Feelings like graceful, delicate flowers: is Nina at this point summoning up those past feelings or is she, in reciting from the play, inadvertently and insensitively crushing Konstantin's heart, tearing those flowers (and his heart) up by the roots? *Just so long as no one . . . tells Mama. It might distress Mama*: the pathos, as well as the absurdity, of this sentiment is intense in view of the distress he is about to cause 'Mama' by killing himself. However, this is the one moment in the play where one person appears to show genuine concern for the feelings of another.

66 *(Gets the stuffed seagull out of the cupboard)*: whether the seagull is depicted in flight or not may be a significant choice that a production has to consider.

No recollection!: it is presumably plausible that Trigorin has no recollection of asking to have the seagull stuffed, but Chekhov seems to be implying that his denial is a failure of imagination as well as one of memory. Trigorin's imaginative capacity seems as limited as his memory, both earthbound and stuffed.

Something in my medicine chest bursting: Chekhov uses the same verb for 'bursting' (lopnut') as he does for the sound of the breaking string in *The Cherry Orchard*. If the latter sound is symbolic so, in an important sense, is this one.

. . . and a few moments later comes back in again: Chekhov's stage direction is very specific. Dorn is offstage for a whole half minute.

(He hums to himself.): Dorn here repeats the words of the Kradin melody from Act One: 'Once again before thee . . .' but he adds the words which were missing earlier, 'stoiu ocharovan', which means 'I stand enchanted'. At this point the 'enchantment', apart from its associations with the lake, perhaps needs to be seen as resembling the princess who pricks her finger with a needle and sleeps for a hundred years. Dorn is 'turned to stone' or alternatively, into a stuffed dummy like the seagull.

From a correspondent in America: America has specific connotations for a Russian. 'To go to America' can be a Russian metaphor for committing suicide, just as 'to discover America' is to say, or disclose, nothing new. In this sense, a correspondent in America is one in the Next, rather than the New, World. Just before blowing his brains out in Dostoevsky's *Crime and Punishment*, the nihilistic Svidrigailov is asked by 'a little man, wrapped in a soldier's grey greatcoat and wearing a copper helmet that made him look like Achilles [. . .] "Vell, vot do you vant here already?"', to which Svidrigailov replies 'I am going [. . .] to America', and produces a revolver. 'But you can't do that here! This is not the proper place!' complains Achilles, but '[Svidrigailov] lifted the revolver to his right temple [and] pulled the trigger' (trans. Jessie Coulson). There may be a deliberate echo at the end of *The Seagull* of this serio-comic moment in Dostoevsky's novel. The naturalistic and undramatic equation of bursting bottles and shattered temples is, however, couched in the limited mode of Trigorin's kind of realistic drama, not Chekhov's. There may also be a connection with the suicide at the end of Ibsen's *Hedda Gabler*, when the judge can only mutter the self-protective credo of bourgeois mores: 'People don't do such things.'

Questions for Further Study

1 The original title page of *The Seagull* describes the play as 'a comedy'. How might you challenge, or justify, the application of the term to this particular play?

2 A prominent theme of *The Seagull* has been described, in the broadest sense, as 'the artist and his or her relationship to their art'. What importance would you place on this notion and why?

3 Critics have been struck by the theme of frustrated love relationships in *The Seagull* where A loves B who does not love A but loves C, etc. How far does this seem to you a significant theme?

4 To what extent is *The Seagull* a play about 'innocence' and 'experience', 'youth' and 'age'?

5 Does an analysis of the final scene between Konstantin and Nina in Act Four of *The Seagull* suggest that she is the positive heroine and he the negative anti-hero of the play?

6 Consider the importance of dysfunctional family relationships and especially father figures in *The Seagull*.

7 To what extent does *The Seagull* deploy the metaphor of theatre to suggest the unreality of life itself?

8 How significant are the themes of 'time' and 'memory' in *The Seagull*?

9 Is Konstantin a symbolist writer and *The Seagull* a symbolist play?

10 Is Trigorin a naturalist writer and *The Seagull* a naturalistic play?

11 How important a part does the natural world, apart from the seagull itself, play in *The Seagull*?

12 What is the significance of 'the play-within-the-play' in *The Seagull*?

13 To what extent does Chekhov's familiarity with Shakespeare's *Hamlet* impinge on *The Seagull* and contribute to your appreciation of the later play?

14 How significant a part do the estate workers and servants, including Shamrayev, play in *The Seagull*?

15 The figure of 'the doctor' in Chekhov's plays is often said to reflect the dramatist's own position, given that he was also a medical practitioner. To what extent would you agree that Dorn is the play's rational reference point in *The Seagull*?

16 Would you agree that the main theme of *The Seagull* is the conflict between 'romantic' and 'realistic' attitudes to life?

17 Does a reading of Stanislavsky's production score for *The Seagull* convince you that his way of staging the play was definitive?

18 How do you explain the almost inconsequential, low-key ending to *The Seagull*?

19 Maurice Valency described *The Seagull* as 'a bitter vaudeville' in the sense of a low farce. What do you think he meant by this and how far would you agree?